TAMING THE TV HABIT

Taming the TV Habit

*How Television Menaces Your
Mind, Marriage, and Family*

Kevin Perrotta

SERVANT BOOKS
Ann Arbor, Michigan

Cover photo by John B. Leidy
Book Design by John B. Leidy

Available from Servant Books, Box 8617,
Ann Arbor, Michigan 48107

Printed in the United States of America
ISBN 0-89283-155-3

Contents

Time To Take Stock

WELCOME TO THE SECOND AGE of television. After only thirty
years, television's first age is drawing to a close. A second
television age, offering a more spectacular display of video
fireworks, has begun.

The first age opened in a half-dozen cities with a few
thousand small, dim television screens mounted in heavy
mahogany cabinets—the puffing steam engines of a new
technological revolution. The first age brought large screens
and sharp, color pictures. A huge entertainment and information industry arose. The biggest audiences in history
gathered. In 1980, more than a billion people around the world
watched a single event—the World Cup soccer finals.

Now, billions of viewing hours later and millions of miles of
celluloid and videotape away from *The Honeymooners* and *You
Are There* (remember Ralph Cramden and Ed Murrow?), we
are leaving behind the First Great Television Experience. With
our sharply focused color screens and remote controls we are
entering the second age, where the number of inputs into our
home sets expands enormously. Cable television, which now
carries up to 36 channels, may soon expand to 150 channels, and
then to 1000. Videodiscs, now an expensive novelty, may
become as cheap and varied as record albums. Viewers' choices
may widen from what's available locally to whatever is broadcast
anywhere in the world and transmitted by satellite. The limited
choice of the network-dominated first Television Age will pass

into history along with intercity passenger rail travel and prime-time evening radio.

The cable and videodisc systems and videotape players of the early and mid 1980's give only a foretaste of what is to come. These are only the preliminary fireworks, set off to gather a crowd. The real show will begin when the audiences reach the critical mass that makes full-scale use of technical possibilities profitable.

Since the main event is yet to come, this is a suitable moment to switch off the set and take a few hours to think about television rather than watch it. Before we hurtle into the world of limitless video, we should consider what we have learned about television so far. How might our experience and our insights so far prepare us for what is to come? That is the purpose of this book—to aid our reflection on the problems and possible uses of television.

Many books and articles have been written about the phenomenon of television, so it may be helpful to say something at the start about what this book will try to do which other articles and books have not done.

This book is a Christian perspective on the use of television in the Christian home. To say that it is a specifically Christian book does not mean that it is: (1) concerned mainly with attacking violence and sex on television; (2) concerned very much with Christian programming; or (3) concerned at all with how Christians can influence what gets broadcast. All of these are important topics for Christians to be concerned about, but this book is not especially concerned with them.

The reason for this is that questioning what is actually seen on television is not the point at which to begin thinking about television's effects and uses. The place to begin is with questions such as, What are we *not doing* because we are watching television? Does the act of watching television affect us differently from other activities, such as reading or playing softball? By asking questions like these, we find that one of television's greatest impacts on our lives is the simple fact that we spend so much time with it. These effects are basically the same whether we are viewing the Metropolitan Opera or the Muppets.

Of course, television content is important, and when we examine it we will discuss violence and sex. But even then, these will not be our chief concern. Violence and sex are not the only, or even the most serious, problems with television programming. The greater problems lie in the ways television nourishes non-Christian patterns of thinking about the world. Many secular groups concerned about television—parent-teacher organizations, doctors' associations, psychologists—have placed violence at the top of their agendas. The fact that Christians have done this too suggests that Christians are having their priorities shaped by secular culture. Violence is only part of the problem. What is more urgent for Christians today is to develop a Christian critique of television's profoundly secular cultural influences on all of us.

This book will not offer a critique of Christian programming because that subject deserves special attention. It is too large a topic to fit comfortably in a book which is basically concerned with how Christians use the largely secular medium of television in our homes. Television will be a predominantly secular medium for many years to come. Thus understanding its effects on us will continue to be very important, no matter how rapidly Christian programming develops. Meanwhile, others have begun to write specifically about programming which is explicitly Christian. For example, see Virginia Stem Owens's *Total Image, Or Selling Jesus in the Modern Age.*[1]

Neither is the present book about how to effect changes in what gets on the air or onto the cable. That too would require a book of its own. Rather our topic here is what we do with what is actually available on the home screen. Christians who are working from outside the television industry for the removal of offensive material, or from within to constructively shape television programming, are engaged in an important public service. This book, however, has a different purpose.

Our goal is to lay the basis for a reasonable Christian use of television which curbs its ill effects and uses it to best advantage. Among the questions we ask are, How do our viewing habits affect Christian family life? the rearing of children? the formation of a Christian mind? Our method will be to reflect on what is known about how television affects our lives, in the light of the Christian faith. Many other works have covered parts of the same ground in more depth and detail, usually from a secular point of view. In this book we have surveyed and sketched the findings of many researchers and observers of television in order to reach practical conclusions about what we ought to do with that appealing, colorful, rude, witty, and time-consuming video companion in all our homes.

ONE

Paying with Our Time

TELEVISION IS ALL AROUND us, but most of the time we do not give it much thought. It shapes our views of politics, our knowledge of sports, our shopping habits. We arrange our living room furniture, our mealtimes and bedtimes, even our bathroom breaks around television. Yet it does not seem to be a particularly important part of our lives. Television remains somewhat difficult to think about or take seriously. There is something elusive about the television experience.

The reason may be that our relationship with television is largely casual. A couple of hours of entertainment in the evening, background babble as we are cooking or cleaning, sights and sounds in the next room keeping the children occupied—all of this has a time-out quality. Despite the occasional magnetic excitement of a bowl game, a first-rate movie, or a presidential debate, television plays a low-key part in our lives. This pastime quality deflects our attempts to think about it seriously. It seems a mistake to make too much of something which is largely cheap entertainment.

This is one of television's peculiarities. It so easily affects our lives so profoundly. In a mere thirty years, North Americans, Europeans, Japanese, and millions of people everywhere in the world have absorbed its transforming presence as readily as a sponge soaks up water. It has happened effortlessly, naturally.

The sponge comparison is instructive. The water filling the empty chambers of the sponge is not exactly occupying a void. It is replacing air. Television also has not simply filled voids in

11

people's lives. It has intruded; it has displaced other things. For all the centuries before 1950, people were not sitting idly in cottage and castle waiting for television to appear. On the contrary, their lives were full of activities—productive and unproductive, social and solitary. Television has displaced some of these activities. Where something else was, now television is.

This fact suggests that we should take a different approach to the effects of television than the one we are used to taking. When we think about television's effects on our lives, we usually focus our attention on the programs' content. The most urgently asked question is whether television makes people, especially children, more aggressive, or violent, or criminal. Parent-teacher guilds, psychologists, ministers, and congressmen have all weighed the question, and professional journals are littered with studies of the subject. A report to the nation's surgeon general in 1972 giving this question primary attention filled 2,330 pages.[1] More recently, as the midcentury sexual revolution has penetrated the world of television entertainment, sex has risen as a matter of concern. Groups like the Moral Majority and the National Coalition for Better Television have launched campaigns to get networks and advertisers to clean up salacious material.

However, the simple issue of television's displacement effects has been left behind in the dust. Some observers of television have given the topic thought, but the issue of television's claim on our time has never emerged as a major item for discussion.

Discussion of television usually assumes that the habits of heavy television viewing which we have adopted are the only possible ones. A radical departure from our heavy time investment with television is inconceivable. Every once in a while we read about how the members of a fundamentalist church in some small town have carted all their television sets off to the dump. But very few of us take such acts seriously.

Yet we must ask this question: What if all the programs on television were innocuous or even, in our judgment, good? Would we be comfortable spending as much time with the medium as we do? Would it be healthy to spend two to three or more hours a day—fourteen to twenty-one or more hours a week—watching television, even if the programs were harmless or even good? Over our lives, that amounts to 50,000 to 75,000 or more hours—five to eight or more years watching the movement of light on the inner surface of a vacuum tube. Surely the expenditure of these five to eight or more years of our lives deserves closer attention.

For most of us in television-viewing societies, an entire viewing life-cycle has come into existence. We begin to watch early in life, and by the age of three we are putting in an hour of viewing a day. Our viewing rises to a preschool peak, then falls off for a couple of years as school takes a significant portion of our time. By the age of seven, however, we have made the adjustment to school, and television watching again assumes an increasing part of our day. This rise climaxes in the years from twelve to fourteen. By our early twenties we enter the mainstream of adult society and settle down to a steady level of television viewing through middle age. With declining physical activity in our fifties and retirement in our sixties, we turn ever more extensively to the television. Finally, a gradual decline in our television viewing accompanies the slowdown of all our mental and physical activities. The years of formal education come and go, the child-bearing and child-rearing time of our lives arrives and departs, our earning capacity expands and shrinks; but, lo, television is with us always.

Heavy television viewing throughout life is becoming a global phenomenon. French sociologists find that their countrymen increasingly take their before-dinner aperitifs at home rather than in the cafe and simplify their cuisine—because of television. The Japanese find themselves as concerned as Americans about the possible effects of heavy childhood viewing on school achievement and social adjustment.

In the Third World the situation is similar. In fact, in some cases, television's intrusion into daily life is more striking than it is in more developed countries. In Latin America, for example, levels of involvement with television in some cases reach

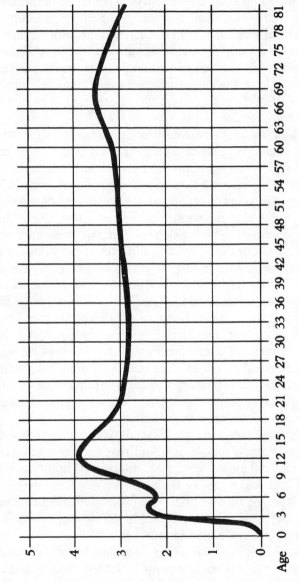

Figure 1. The Lifetime Television-Viewing Cycle

The chart is a composite representation of various studies. Some researchers would put the entire line higher, some lower. There is general agreement, however, on the shape of the curve—a couple of peaks in childhood, a decline in the teens, a steady pattern in adulthood until retirement, when there is another rise.

startling heights. A survey by the University of Chile found that many domestic servants, city housewives, and older single women watched fifty or more hours of television each week.[2] Television is increasingly available even to people who are quite poor, often through communal neighborhood ownership. By the end of the 1980's almost everyone in the world may have access to a television set.

Society after society seems to follow a similar path. In each nation, the average daily viewing time of those who have television rises as the percentage of television owners grows. Then, as almost everyone in the society comes to own a television set, the average daily viewing time for set owners reaches a certain limit and levels off.[3] Television assumes a stable, substantial place in everyone's lives—two to three or more hours per day. In the United States we reached our plateau around 1970. Since then our level of viewing has not changed appreciably.

Life on the viewing plateau means leisure-time saturation. We have become accustomed to a certain daily television intake, and our viewing habits do not appear to be affected much by the variety of offerings or what we think of them. On the one hand, daily viewing time does not seem to rise as more channels become available. On the other hand, growing dissatisfaction with television fare does not seem to drive us from our screens. One study found that between 1960 and 1980 the "percentage of viewers who consider commercial television programs un-informative has tripled from 7 to 21; those who believe them often in bad taste increased from 13 to 35 percent."[4] But the average viewing figure held steady nonetheless. Another researcher discovered that viewer dissatisfaction was actually rising between 1960 and 1970, the decade during which average daily viewing was completing the rise to its plateau. People with higher levels of education seem to have a lower regard for television programming, but highly educated Americans never-theless watch as much television as everyone else.[5]

We watch television largely because it is part of our daily routine. While we may turn the set on to catch a particular program—and turn it off because we dislike a program—we generally turn the television on and leave it on simply because it is the time in our daily routine to do so. Television watching is thus similar to eating. We eat three meals a day because we have accepted this as the best pattern. If something tasty is around at some other time, we will eat it, and we may occasionally skip a meal. But in general we eat breakfast, lunch, and dinner every day when it is time to eat, regardless of whether we especially like what is available.

The television networks know that television viewing is a matter of habit rather than an action we give much thought to. Their research departments have discovered that people tend to leave the television dial set to a particular channel instead of flipping it to look for better programs. This is why the networks try to avoid airing an unpopular program at the beginning of the evening. Viewers flee to other stations—and stay there all night.

The strength of the television habit was indicated by the findings of two researchers who sought to determine whether decreased television watching led to an increase in family communication. They contacted local television repair shops to get the names of people who were having their televisions fixed. The researchers assumed that these people would be doing without television for a week or so, and they planned to question these families to see if they talked more with the television gone. However, the assumption turned out to be wrong. When people put their set in for repair, they wheeled out a second set from the children's bedroom or borrowed an extra one from friends. The researchers concluded, "For family communication to go up substantially, apparently the household must be totally without television, and that is becoming a rare situation."[6]

The television habit is strong, but the viewing experience remains casual. While the television set is on for an average of more than seven hours a day in American homes, it is not always being looked at with great attention. Television often provides a background for other activities such as balancing the checkbook, doing homework, cooking, and so on. Also, even when we are sitting before the screen, we are often somewhat distracted. One researcher reported: "Of all programs seen . . . between 30 and 40 percent were not watched from beginning to end. Very nearly the same percentage reported engaging in [other] activities while viewing, with conversation being a particularly prevalent distracting activity while viewing (half of such conversations do not refer to the content on the screen). Another 30 to 40 percent . . . were unable to give an accurate recount of what the programs last seen were all about."[7] There are indications that as the years go by, people watch television less intensively, though for no less total hours. However, even when television does not claim our full attention, it affects our mood and relationships. One researcher noted that "when television was being viewed with members of the family, in contrast to being with the family without TV, subjects reported feeling significantly less challenged, less skilled, more relaxed, less alert, less strong, and less active."[8]

Thus television is an activity both deeply embedded in our lives and often of an aimless and low-involvement quality. Sometimes it is hard to say whether television is distracting us from other things, or other things are distracting us from television. But television viewing affects other activities in either case—both when it operates in an intense, attention-grabbing mode and when it functions as a pervasive low-interest diversion.

So here we are, spending several years of our lives watching television. This brings us back to the question we asked at first: Instead of what? We are making a massive investment of our time watching the patterns created by streams of electrons on the inside of a cathode ray tube. What else could we be doing? Reading? Talking? Fixing the roof or playing softball or sitting on the porch? Thinking, or praying?

The question is important because the investment is so great. The only way to determine whether we are making a wise investment of our time—that is, of ourselves—is to consider what other things we might be doing, and what rewards we might get from doing them. To know whether all those

© 1981 Punch/Rothco

*"This design of memorial stone is
very popular, sir."*

thousands of hours sitting in front of the screen are worth it, we
need to know more than whether we are getting *some* return. We
need to know whether we are getting the *best* return.

In other words we need to ask whether watching television
may be costing us the opportunity to do other things that in the
long run might make us better and happier people, other things
that God might want us to do.

Business people recognize the cost of lost opportunities. Even
a profitable venture can involve an opportunity cost that is so
high that the venture should not be undertaken. The managers
of the Make-a-Bag Company may know that the company can
realize a ten percent profit by expanding operations into the

manufacture of plastic bags. But before they decide to make plastic bags, they will investigate other ways to use their resources. What if producing cardboard boxes would yield a fifteen percent profit? If making plastic bags prevented them from making boxes, the company would forego an additional five percent return. Even with the possible ten percent profit, the managers might decide that plastic-bag manufacture involved a prohibitive opportunity cost.

Every decision to put time and money into one course of action closes off the opportunity to put that time and money into another. The principle applies as much to how we live as to how companies make business decisions. It applies equally to making bags and raising a family.

With this in mind, then, let us attempt to calculate the opportunity cost of our television viewing. Of course, there will be no way to put a numerical value on it. It is impossible to measure precisely how much satisfaction we derive from our viewing or to put a figure on what we lose. We can, however, consider the advantages and disadvantages, and weigh them according to the overall goals we have for our lives.

TWO

Displacement Effects

FOR THE SAKE of argument, let us grant that television watching is a profitable experience in it own terms. We watch television primarily to be entertained, to escape, to relax. Since we continue to watch day after day, it only makes sense to conclude that we actually *are* being entertained. We also watch to stay in touch with the rest of the world, to be informed, to be in the know. Television accomplishes this too. The entertainment and information have shortcomings. But let us leave these aside at the moment. To some extent—each of us must judge how much—television viewing is successful.

The next question then is, what do we not do because we are watching? Some observers suggest that we would not be doing much of anything. There are those, one newspaper columnist wrote some years ago, "who believe that, take away television, people would read their Bibles, learn Spanish, or create great art." More likely, he thought, they would "make nuisances of themselves." In his view, "persons who are consuming *Let's Make a Deal* and Alistair Cooke with indiscriminate mindlessness are not aggravating the crime rate, occupying beach parking, or lined up in front of you at McDonald's."[1]

There is some point to that. Some of the time we spend watching television we would not otherwise be spending very usefully. We might be arguing with our husband or wife, or brooding over the injustices we have suffered at our job. It is worth noting, however, that some activities which we might consider aimless or undesirable—daydreaming or correcting

21

the children, for example—turn out on closer examination to have some purpose after all.

Clearly, however, television viewing is displacing more than daydreaming. For one thing, we make less use of other forms of mass communication. We spend less time reading newspapers, magazines, and books. We do not listen to the radio as much. We go to the movies less often. This is a simple trade-off. We are substituting one form of mass-produced entertainment and information for other forms.

This is not all. Television displaces more than other forms of mass communication. Since the arrival of television, we spend on an average at least an extra hour and a quarter per day with the mass media.[2] This increase amounts to about nine hours per week, and it is entirely attributable to television. In other words, television has displaced not only listening to the radio and reading newspapers but many other activities as well.

At least three kinds of evidence indicate that daily life activities suffer because of our television viewing. One kind of evidence comes from studies of changes in people's habits when they get television sets. For example, a study in England in the 1950s showed that as people bought television sets, both their interest and participation in a wide variety of educational and recreational activities declined sharply for the first couple of years. Six years after getting their sets, people's interests and participation in other activities were still lower than in pre-television days.[3]

The second kind of evidence comes from studies of what we do when we turn off the set because we do not like what is on. One researcher reported the following results as displayed in Figure 2 (see page 24).[4]

These findings indicate that there is plenty to do when the set is off. Each of us will use our time differently, but these figures show some interesting and useful possibilities. Taking care of home and children and other forms of recreation seem to be leading possibilities for many of us.

The third kind of evidence for what we would be doing if we were not viewing comes from studies of what people do when they turn off their sets completely for a week or so. Such studies are rare because not many people are willing to take part in them. A researcher at Texas Tech University tried to overcome this reluctance by offering to pay people a few dollars a day. Even with this incentive, interviewers had to call two to four people before each participant was recruited.

The results of his study are shown in Figure 3 (see page 24).[2]

This is how we pay for the time spent with television. To reap the entertainment and information benefits, we forego some conversation over the breakfast table with husband or wife about the day ahead, some questions with the children in the afternoon about how school went, a visit with a relative, an evening church activity. Evening church activities? Few of us are old enough to remember the pre-radio days when the church was a real center of social activity. The fact is that television's spread in the 1950s drained attendance from Wednesday prayer meetings and Thursday choir practice and put week-long parish missions out of business.

Paying for television with our time thus means diminishing the time and attention we give to the people toward whom we have some kind of responsibility—our spouse, children, fellow Christians, relatives, people in need. Television allures us and distracts us from other things we should be thinking about or doing. This amounts to quite a price, when we pay it to the tune of two to three or more hours a day. Let us consider the consequences in a little detail.

Husbands and wives need time to talk. There is an apartment or house to be cared for, children to raise, money to spend, and—well, the point is obvious. One does not have to take a sentimental view of marriage—husband and wife sharing every passing emotional tingle or shadow—to see the practical need for good, honest talk between spouses. Every marriage counselor will testify to that.

Many husbands and wives, however, do not communicate well with each other. Television is hardly the only reason or even the main one. And even where television plays a part in muffling communication between spouses, it is more often a

Figure 2. Activities when Television Is Turned Off

Alternative Activity when the Television Is Turned Off	Percent of Total
Work	4
Housework and child care	27
Shopping and personal care (sleeping, eating, etc.)	9
Study and homework	4
Organizational activity	3
Entertainment and visiting	6
Other leisure	28
Other	3
No answer, don't know	16

Figure 3. Activities with and without Television

Activity	Week with Television (in minutes)	Week without Television (in minutes)
Involvement with newspapers, books, magazines, etc.	86	175
Social activities with friends	72	118
Household chores	82	101
Social activities with immediate family	42	70

means of escape from one's partner rather than the *cause* of the flight from communication. But certainly one obstacle to better communication is simply lack of time.

"Charles, why didn't we talk about our plans before we came up here for our vacation?" "Why didn't you tell me before that you were having a hard time during the day taking care of David?" "I am really annoyed that Rick hasn't let me know what his thinking is about where the children should go to school next year." The reason for problems like these is often that husband and wife have not taken the time to sit down and talk. There has been too much going on.

When we find ourselves dealing with communication problems with our spouse, we might ask ourselves whether it is *true* that there has been no time to talk. What about the two to three or more hours a day we may be spending with television?

Of course, husbands and wives and everyone else talk while they are watching televison. But a good deal of our television viewing is not accompanied by much conversation. If we miss something in the program, we have no way of bringing the scene back. So the more we happen to be interested in television, the less friendly we feel about interruptions, even less than when we are reading the sports page or an exciting book. So when we are viewing with our spouse, we are involved in a common activity but often in a way that is parallel rather than interactive—that is, without communicating.

Not everyone who watches a lot of television is failing to deal with immediate responsibilities to someone else. It may be that we simply have time on our hands. This is the case with many younger, single men and women, for example. It is also true of many older people: one's sphere of responsibilities has contracted; the physical abilities to do things and get around are reduced. Time hangs heavy. Thankfully, it seems, there is television.

However, television watching may be a problem even if we are not neglecting other things we ought to be doing. The time spent before the screen may be a way of dealing with tension or anxiety, difficulties with family members, purposelessness and boredom, fears of other people or loneliness. To give just one example, researchers have found that children who are heavy television viewers also tend to have more difficulties in social situations. They are not as adaptable, outgoing, and do not make as many friends. In such cases, television viewing may not be causing the problems, but rather may be a way of compensating for them.[6]

Tensions, boredom, loneliness, and so on have been around for a long time, but they are particularly common in our society today. Our society puts us more on our own, at every period of life, than was true, say, of people a hundred years ago. Families are not so closely knit, people are not so interdependent, individuals are more mobile. Along with the advantages to these changes, there are disadvantages—among them, a greater incidence of emotional and relational problems. Indications of this are all around us in climbing rates of alcohol and drug abuse, suicide rates, and other depressing signs that many people's lives are not working very well.

Television fits into a pattern of activities which provide temporary relief from the difficulties our society tends to produce. It is a technological fix to the problems of a technological society. Television relaxes the tense, momentarily stimulates the purposeless, entertains the bored, offers escape to the unselfconfident, is a companion to the lonely.

What viewing does not do, however, is to help us actually deal with the causes of our tension, social fears, loneliness, or whatever problem we may be escaping by viewing. On the contrary, television is like a drug—which is why Marie Winn entitled her insightful book on television *The Plug-In Drug*. Possibly for some people—shut-ins, for instance—television watching may be all they can do for much of the day. But surely, for everyone, drugs that mask the symptoms rather than treat the causes should be taken carefully. If we are investing substantial amounts of time in television watching, we should ask ourselves how else we might use our time to get at the roots of the difficulties which television helps us escape.

Television watching may be a more serious act of escape—from God. When is there time to lift our minds and hearts to God? When are there quiet moments in our busy coming-and-going days to read scripture, to ponder the meaning of a single verse for us, to refresh ourselves with reading a spiritual book? In the psalms we glimpse the daily lives of men and women aware of God throughout days which must have been busy with the ordinary tasks of life. "Morning by morning, O Lord, you hear my voice." "I have set the Lord always before me." "Even at night my heart instructs me." "When I awake, I will be satisfied with seeing your likeness." In the psalms we hear men and women in their daily lives—sometimes in the temple but sometimes at home, in the fields, in the middle of problems—turning their attention toward God. When is there time for prayer to break forth from us? Perhaps there is little time because we prefer the banter of a news-and-chatter program in the morning. Perhaps we have other images before us. Perhaps when we awake we are content to see other likenesses.

Not all our viewing distracts us from uninterrupted prayer. Maybe we could not have been alone anyway for the few minutes we spent watching the morning television talk show or the hour we watched a police adventure in the evening. In the morning we were getting ready for work; in the evening we were spending time with the family. Even so, television may be displacing something akin to prayer—the opportunity to reflect on our experience, to remember a word of God's, to consider how he wants us to handle a situation. Thought can verge on prayer and cross over into it. The psalmist asks, "May the meditation of my heart be pleasing in your sight, O Lord." It is unnaturally self-conscious to expect to have pious, spiritual subjects constantly running through our minds. But there is nothing superspiritual in wanting to have our thoughts please God. It is perfectly reasonable to turn our thoughts to consider him and our responsibilities in light of his word. When can this happen? The in-between moments when we are waiting for the toast to pop or sitting in the living room after dinner are prime opportunities. If we let the lights and sounds of television flood all such moments, we are closing off the natural opportunities simply to think.

Television's displacement effects spread in so many directions that one researcher has called it the single greatest rearranger of people's time in the twentieth century. Among the many aspects of life that our viewing habits have affected are three overlapping sets of relationships: extended family, neighborhood, and church. For various reasons these relationships are not doing very well in our society. Television is far from being the main cause, but it contributes to the trend.

In general, few of us have the close family ties outside the nuclear family that many people had in the past. Some people are exceptions. A friend of mine from a Sicilian-American family in New York jointly owns a business with his three brothers and often gets together with relatives who live throughout the New York City area. For business and pleasure the members of the family see one another often. But increasingly for most of us, many relatives reside in distant parts of the country, live different lives, and do not take a great deal of responsibility for one another. Television adds its weight to this pattern. Instead of visiting with relatives who *are* close by, out of duty or simply for something to do, we tend to stay home and watch television. Our relatives do too. (Television's influence on extended families is not all bad, one researcher claims. He believes that family reunions are more peaceful with television because family members are able to focus their attention on the television rather than on each other, and thus avoid arguments and unpleasantness!)

A woman writing about the disintegration of a Jewish neighborhood in the Bronx after World War II noted the great impact the arrival of television had. Her neighbors spent less time sitting out on the front steps, visiting with one another in the grocery, or walking in the local park in the evening. She saw this as the first stage in the weakening sense of neighborhood which culminated finally in its destruction. Her reminiscences could equally well describe what has happened in many other cities and towns. Other factors more important than television are at work in the break-up of the old-fashioned neighborhoods where people knew one another well, spent time socializing, and relied on each other for various kinds of help. But television has an impact on neighborhood relationships because most of the time we spend with our neighbors is free time, time when we are somewhat at loose ends. Spending time with neighbors hardly seems a high priority, so it easily gives way to television. Certainly for most of us spending time with the neighbors is not important enough to keep us from watching television, which is even less demanding an activity than talking to the lady next door.

Television's subtraction of time from relatives and neighbors may make our lives easier. But ultimately it makes us poorer. When we consider television's effects on our church relationships, we confront an even more important issue. The call to Christian discipleship leads us together with fellow Christians. God intends to bring us into a full experience of his life as we learn to serve him *together*. Scripture is full of phrases which describe the bond we have as fellow Christians. We are "brothers and sisters" in Christ. We are in "fellowship" with God and each other. We belong to "one body."

It would take us far beyond the topic of this book to explore the nature of Christians' relationship with one another in Christ, or why Christians' relationships today fall so far short of the scriptural ideal. But clearly our relationships with other Christians are important, and clearly television has contributed to weakening these ties. In the church as elsewhere, television is not the main force behind the breakdown of people's relationships. Rather it quickens the processes of isolation and anesthetizes us to them. It also distracts us from the opportunities to serve the many needy people who are around us if we would take the time to look for them.

A twist of the television switch to off would not instantly recreate our relationships as Christians. The sources of renewal in the church lie elsewhere—in a deeper understanding of Christians' relationship with one another as scripture portrays

it, in wise pastoral leadership, in the working of the Holy Spirit. Nevertheless it is necessary to grasp how television viewing fits in. Sooner or later we will have to face the large amounts of time invested in television watching as an obstacle to church renewal.

We have been considering adult concerns—how television viewing replaces talking, developing relationships and dealing with problems, praying and thinking. There are also concerns when it comes to children. Some people say that television's effects are greater for children than adults. This is arguable, since we spend most of our five to eight or more years before the screen in adulthood. But certainly television's displacement effects on children deserve special consideration. As we have noted, viewing is very heavy during childhood, which is when our lives are being deeply formed.

How has television affected child-rearing? Most parents allow their children to watch a great deal of television. This removes an opportunity for children to learn how to relate to other people, and replaces it with an opportunity to learn how to sit and watch light. An opportunity to train children in basic social skills in one's own home is exchanged for the opportunity to have one's children's minds fed images crafted on Sunset Boulevard.

Heavy television viewing contributes to parents' movement to the periphery of their children's lives. Kas Kalba notes: "The trend away from direct parental involvement in the socialization of children is not a new one. Both the increasing separation of home and work place and the increasing formalization of schooling have served to limit parental supervision of the social and emotional development of the young. Television, however, has reinforced this tendency. For now even those limited moments when parent and child are together in the home are subject to the competitive appeal of the TV set (or radio, or record player, or telephone)."[7]

As Kalba points out, aspects of contemporary life already narrow the time which parents have with their children. One or both parents are gone from home during the daytime most of the week. Children are gone to school. It was not always this way—as I was reminded recently on a visit to Greenfield Village, an outdoor museum in Dearborn, Michigan. One exhibit there is an old English blacksmith's shop, transported and reassembled, which was operated continuously for almost 300 years by the men of one family. Generation after generation the men worked the smithy near their home and trained their boys to take over the business. This arrangement gave fathers and sons a great deal of time together. In centuries past, working in farms and workshops and in the home, fathers and mothers naturally were with the boys and girls for much of the day. We parents have much shorter stretches of time with our sons and daughters. This is a necessary price we pay for our technological culture. The food, medical care, and material goods which make us more advantaged than those seventeenth-century blacksmiths involve a lifestyle which gives us less time with our children. Realizing this should stimulate us to make the most of the time we have. Unfortunately, in practice, as Kalba points out, "the competitive appeal of the TV set severely reduces this opportunity."

Less parental training means ill-trained children. If we are not willing to spend time teaching our children how to play peacefully with one another, do household chores, handle money, show respect for other people, and care for their possessions, then we will have children and, later, adults who are weak in qualities of cooperativeness, diligence, responsibility, and general maturity.

In raising children, we make few single decisions of great importance. What matters is the accumulation of small decisions we make day by day. Every day we decide how we will spend time with our children. Day by day, evening by evening, many of us choose to watch television and let our children watch it. By doing so we are choosing certain outcomes for them, for ourselves, for the church, and for society.

Marie Winn has written perceptively: "The more direct forms of parental love require time and patience, steady, dependable, ungrudgingly given time actually spent *with* a child, reading to him, comforting him, playing, joking, and working with him. But even if a parent were eager and willing to demonstrate that sort of direct love to his children today, the opportunities are diminished. What with school and Little League and piano lessons and, of course, the inevitable television programs, a day seems to offer just enough time for a good-night kiss."[8]

Winn discerns a chain of causes and effects. The absorption of parent-child time by television viewing reduces parental training, leading to undisciplined children, leading to mothers' increasing impatience with domestic life. She writes of

parents' steady loss of control as they withdraw from an active role in their children's upbringing. . . . As the parents grow less powerful, they discover themselves less and less capable of coping with their strong but undisciplined, grumpy, threatening children. Common sense suggests that without television, parents would have been unable to survive life under such circumstances; they would have been *forced* to socialize their children more persistently, *forced* to work a little harder at making them speak more agreeably or behave more considerately. But television . . . abolishes the need to establish these sorts of disciplines. There is no longer the impetus to ensure the sort of behavior that would allow a mother to cook dinner or talk on the telephone or assert herself in any way without being eaten alive, in a manner of speaking, by her children. . . .

Of course, the Women's Liberation movement has played a major role in leading mothers away from a life of child care and domestic responsibilities. But it does not seem unlikely that the increased willfulness, demandingness, and disagreeableness of undisciplined children makes a life of staying home seem less appealing than the drabbest, most routine office job so many women choose in exchange.[9]

Time spent watching television not only reduces opportunities for training children. It also interferes with children's education. Since the mid-seventies educators have been worried by indications that children are not learning as much as children in the past. The average scores of the nation's high school juniors and seniors on Scholastic Aptitude Tests—standardized tests used by college admissions offices to evaluate applicants—began to decline in 1962. In 1975 the College Entrance Examinations Board, which designs the tests, concluded after investigation that the drop in scores represented an actual weakening in students' "developed reasoning ability." The drop could not be traced to changes in the tests, to changes in the social class of the students taking the tests, or to other factors.[10]

By the late 1970s, not only were the average national SAT scores declining but the number of students who posted scores in the highest range also began to fall. In 1972, of about one million high school seniors who took the verbal SAT, 53,974 scored 650 points or better out of 800 points. In 1980, of a similar number of seniors, 29,019 scored in the 650 to 800-point range—a drop of 46 percent. In the same period, there was a drop of 22 percent in the number of seniors scoring 650 points or more in the math SAT. Richard Berendzen, president of American University, in Washington, D.C., commented, "There is a very small percentage of people, probably just 1 or 2 percent, who have the ability to make really extraordinary contributions. We seem not to be developing this pool of talent as well as we did in the past."[11]

Other signs began to point downward. A federally funded testing organization called the National Assessment of Educational Progress discovered educational regress. It found in the middle of the seventies that junior and senior high school students knew less about science than students at the beginning of the decade.[12] For a nation with one of the world's most elaborate and expensive educational establishments, a nation which depends for its survival and prosperity on the professional and technical competence of large numbers of its citizens, these were disturbing reports. Had the educational process shifted into reverse? Certainly here was strong evidence to support what many teachers and parents had been saying for some time—discipline, concentration, logical reasoning abilities, and other intellectual skills were waning.

Educators were not slow to finger television as the culprit. All those mindless hours watching shoot-outs and cereal commercials, they argued, couldn't be good for anyone's mental development. The main argument was that opportunities were being lost. Children were in front of the tube rather than curled up with a book. The results were less studiousness, less learning, lower scholastic aptitude scores, reduced knowledge of science. Professional educators such as Fred Hargadon, Stanford University's dean of admissions, simply noted, "This is the first generation of students most affected by the media revolution," that is, by television.

The charge that television viewing is damaging young

people's academic performance has now been tested. As with other accusations directed at television, a three-fold set of conclusions emerges:

1. The charges seem to have been overstated.

2. It is difficult to *prove* a cause and effect relationship between television viewing and poorer school performance because there are so many other variable factors.

3. There *is* solid evidence that television has a limited but real adverse effect on school performance.

"The rationale for conjecturing a negative television effect on [academic] achievement," writes Robert C. Hornik of Stanford University, "relies on the notion of displacement. Use of the medium replaces other activities. Time spent with television interferes with homework and serious study; heavy viewers go to bed late and cannot concentrate on schoolwork ; television addicts do not read or follow other more 'educational'" pursuits."[13] What is the evidence that this is so?

Numerous studies have tried to answer this question. Some have not found any significant relationship between children's grades and test scores and their viewing time. Findings early in the television age which indicated that heavy viewing went hand in hand with lower grades have been called into question by later researchers who have criticized the early testing methods as inadequate. As the years have gone by, there is some indication that the difference in academic performance between light and heavy viewers is narrowing, probably because all children, at every level of academic attainment, now watch a lot of television.

Some studies have indicated that brighter children tend to be heavier television consumers than slower children. If so, these children might be even more successful in school if they watched less television. Nevertheless, this finding does not support the contention that heavy viewing is a cause of poor school performance.[14]

These varied and even contradictory studies suggest that claims that television is destroying children's abilities to do well in school have been exaggerated. If the relationship were as

clear and strong as some people say it is, we would expect the
relationship to show up less ambiguously in research. However,
there do seem to be good reasons for linking poorer performance
in school and heavier television viewing, even though these
studies do not demonstrate a direct causal relationship.

For example, in a large study of more than 2,000 adolescents,
Leo Hendry and Helen Patrick, of Aberdeen, Scotland, concluded that there were two distinguishable groups of students.
One group consisted of heavy viewers, who also tended to have
low interest in school, a desire to begin working as soon as
possible, less involvement in sports, a greater interest in popular
music, and to be more personally withdrawn. The other group
watched television less. They were also more academically
motivated and less eager to leave school, more active in sports,
less interested in popular music, and had stronger relationships.
Hendry and Patrick concluded that heavy television watching
tended to *fit into* the lives of young people with certain kinds of
dispositions—including a disposition away from schoolwork—
but that heavy television viewing could not be shown to be the
cause of lower academic performance.[15]

A study of Japanese children reached similar conclusions.
Takeo Furu and his associates found that heavy television
viewers had lower school achievement, but that this seemed to
be due to predispositions such as differences in intelligence,
creativity, adaptability, and so on. In other words, children who
were less gifted for schoolwork tended naturally to prefer to
watch television more than those who had greater intellectual
gifts.[16]

In a review of twenty-five years of studies of the relationship
between school achievement and television viewing, Hornik
wrote that "most of the researchers have concluded that the
effects of televiewing are either nonexistent or slightly
negative."[17] If nothing else, this conclusion shows how difficult
it can be to pin down the exact consequences of television's
displacement effects. It is easier to show what television is
displacing than to show the consequences of the displacement.
However, several signs point to heavy viewing as at least a

partial cause of poorer academic performance.

First, while brighter *younger* children tend to be heavier viewers, the pattern changes as children grow older. Elementary school children who do well in school tend to be among the heavier viewers, but the brightest and most creative high school children do not tend to watch a lot of television. This suggests that as children mature there is an overall relationship between less television viewing and superior academic performance.[18]

Second, studies such as Hendry's and Patrick's and Furu's suggest that heavy television viewing leads to lowered performance in school. Children who were not doing well in school in the first place seemed, as a consequence, to develop heavier viewing habits. It is quite reasonable to think that their heavy television watching then reinforced attitudes and patterns that kept them from doing better in school.

Third, a careful study by Hornik provides solid evidence that at least in some circumstances a cause and effect relationship exists between television viewing and slower scholastic development. Hornik studied the academic progress of several groups of children over a four-year period in El Salvador in the 1970s. Some of the children's families had televisions during the whole time. Some did not have television at all. Some bought televisions during the study. Hornik compared the progress of the three groups, and found that children whose families acquired televisions during the study did not make the progress they would have been expected to make in school.

In particular Hornik concluded that "there is a striking negative association of television exposure with long-term reading skills." In other words, the introduction of television was definitely a cause of a long-term slowdown in the children's progress in reading. Since reading is a basic ability for every field of study, the research suggests that television watching would have a detrimental effect on the children's overall performance in school. Hornik's study found some evidence to support this also.[19]

The degree to which television seemed to affect reading progress was not very large—about ten percent. However, considering the crucial importance of reading, should parents allow their children to fall ten percent behind where they would otherwise have been in the development of their reading skills? Over a twelve-year basic education, a ten-percent loss amounts to more than a year of academic development.

Our investigation of viewing and school performance illustrates some things about the nature of television's effects. The effects of television viewing are always mingled with other factors. Rarely are its effects clear cut. It is not easy to demonstrate with certainty that television causes particular problems or to measure the degree to which it does. Research regarding television, while voluminous, is sometimes contradictory or at least far short of being conclusive.

This offers a reminder that while television is a major component of our lives, it is still relatively new and many questions about its long-term effects on us remain to be answered. Until they are, we have to apply a certain amount of common sense. We cannot wait fifty years for the social scientists to agree that particular effects of television have been demonstrated. Rather we need to consider what can be learned from the scientists now, and draw reasonable conclusions about how we should handle the medium.

For example, it is reasonable to suspect, from our experience and from numerous studies, that heavy television viewing interferes with acquisition of reading skills. While the scientists will continue investigating the question further, parents have sufficient evidence now to take action to ensure that their children do not pay an academic opportunity cost for heavy television viewing.

Our survey of the opportunities lost while we sit in front of our television screens has produced a substantial list. Television is a subtraction, or at least a distraction, from talking with our spouse, children, and others who are close to us. It anesthetizes us to problems such as tension and loneliness, diverting us from seeking real solutions. It fills our time with an endless cascade of pictures and sounds, engaging our attention when we would otherwise have moments for reflection, study, and prayer. From its central place in our living and family rooms, television's displacement effects ripple out into our larger families, neighborhoods, and churches. Within our homes, television places itself between parents and children and between children and reading. This weakens both parental training and intellectual learning, which are crucial if children are to grow up into mature, competent, Christian men and women.

Our heavy investment in television viewing squanders our time. It is a bad deal. What we gain in entertainment and information does not compensate us for what we lose in terms of ordinary life. Whatever our state in life, we have people to care for, things to learn, responsibilities to carry out, God to worship and listen to. If our lives and duties are important, the time we are given to live and carry out our duties must also be important. So we should invest our time wisely. We should get a good return on it.

It could be argued that the television industry values our time and attention more highly that we do ourselves. Each year in the United States billions of dollars are spent on television advertising precisely to win a few minutes of our time. Large corporations are willing to pay hundreds of thousands of dollars for an hour program that will give them the chance to have about five minutes of our time. The current market value of the American people's time, as actually paid for by television advertisers, only suggests the value of our time. It cannot measure the importance of our time to our wife, husband, son, daughter, neighbor, fellow church member, or fellow human being in need—let alone our creator himself.

Our examination of the opportunity of watching television leads us to this conclusion: We need to bring our use of time into closer alignment with our priorities in life. A legitimate goal is to use some of our time for entertainment and information about the world around us. Television is a suitable means to do this. However, we have other goals too—a happy marriage, successfully raising our children, growth as servants of God. By draining away our time, television slows or halts our progress toward these goals. We do not need to eliminate television from our lives but to right this imbalance. We need a wiser use of time. We need a new pattern which satisfies our needs for entertainment and information while not interfering with the other purposes we ought to accomplish. Most of us need simply to spend less time watching television and to spend more time on other things.

THREE

The Empty Experience

IN 1946, AMERICANS were returning to peacetime life—finishing an interrupted education, buying a home, starting a family. Some new elements were going to be part of the postwar world. One, which a few people had seen but most had only heard about, was television.

Television industry pioneer Thomas Hutchinson peered into the future to give everyone an idea of what they could expect. "Today we stand poised on the threshold of a future for television that no one can begin to comprehend fully. We are aware of some of its possibilities, but we are a long, long way from knowing what eventually may be done. We do know, however, that the outside world can be brought into the home, and thus one of mankind's long-standing ambitions has been achieved. You in your home will see events of national importance just as they happen. Personalities that we only hear today will be seen as well as heard tomorrow."[1]

Hutchinson's words point our attention anew to the remarkable nature of television. What was always only dreamed of—instant long-distance visual communication—has become possible and familiar. The marvelous has become ordinary. Yet if we look closely, what has become familiar *remains* marvelous and somewhat mysterious. After more than thirty-five years of study we are still only beginning to understand what is taking place as we and millions of other people sit before our televisions eating corn chips, doing homework, and casually achieving "one of mankind's long-standing ambitions." We are

41

still, in Hutchinson's phrase, "a long, long way from knowing" thoroughly what is going on when we sit watching television, and what its long-term effects may be on us and the generations that will follow us.

Some of what we know—and do not know—concerns the effects of *what* we see on television, that is, the content of the programs. Those effects form the subject of later chapters. In the present chapter, however, we will consider some aspects of the act of viewing itself. What are we doing when we watch television? We are doing something stranger and perhaps more transforming than we may have thought.

With most of our daily television viewing, we are seeking to relax and be entertained. In such a frame of mind, we are largely passive. In fact, television viewing is passive to a greater degree than almost any other form of entertainment.

Viewing television is more passive than other nonparticipative types of entertainment. The stadium crowd watches the football players grind each other into the mud. The reader of the novel sips his drink while the protagonist crawls through barbed wire and artillery fire. But these are not entirely passive activities. The crowd plays a part; it roars its approval and dismay, and in some way adds to the event. After all, what would it be like for two teams to play in a vacant stadium? The reader of the novel proceeds at his own pace, picturing the story to himself, occasionally looking back for a forgotten detail.

The television viewer does none of these things. Unlike the crowd at the game, he is absent to the players. Unlike the reader, he need not imagine anything to himself. In fact, the constantly changing scene before him (the scene shifts on an average at least once every five seconds) makes it difficult to maintain any coherent stream of thought of his own. He is carried along by the program at its own rapid pace. Any physical or mental exertions by the viewer actually distract him from receiving what is being presented. The ideal viewer is receptive, open. Television is described by the old McDonald's jingle: they do it all for you.

Of course, this is to oversimplify. Some programs make

mental demands on the viewer to solve the mystery, anticipate the outcome, follow the line of argumentation, evaluate the performance. But when we are viewing in order to relax and be entertained, which is our major reason for viewing, we naturally choose the programs that require the least mental effort. Watching them we tend to drift into an absorption with the lighted screen that at least dampens mental alertness.

The passivity of viewing is somewhat offset by the fact that we do much of our viewing with other people, making comments and even conversation that may be totally unrelated to what is on the screen. Noting this, one researcher declared that television watching is a surprisingly active rather than passive kind of behavior. However, while viewing is often *accompanied* by activities ranging from sibling squabbles to taking a bath, the act of viewing *itself* is inherently passive. There is no getting around the fact that when we are watching television rather than being distracted from it, we are receiving—receiving only what is being telecast, at the pace it is being telecast.

Many questions might be asked about this passivity, but one which is almost never raised is, "How relaxing is this, really?" The question arises because generally it is not passivity that we find relaxing but activity in a different mode from the one we have been functioning in.

The normal way to relax one muscle is to contract the opposing one (there are muscle-relaxing drugs too, but we do not consider them normal). It is contrasting activity rather than inactivity that relaxes. For relaxation office workers play raquetball, factory workers go fishing, housewives get out of the house.

This natural dynamic suggests that there is something essentially dissatisfying about television as relaxation, at least in large doses. The mental and physical inactivity of television watching deprives it of the ability to produce many of the benefits of more active forms of relaxation. Watching television does not tone up any muscles or prepare us for the satisfying sleep that follows physical exertion. Reading, hobbies, sports,

music, conversation—all have at least the possibility of con-
ferring a sense of accomplishment for knowledge gained,
projects completed, opponents beaten, friendships nourished,
fears overcome, skills acquired. Of course we must choose
recreation wisely. A man may play the horses every night of the
week and never achieve any of these satisfactions—and suffer
some losses too. But to rely on television for relaxation is to
deprive ourselves of most of the ordinary benefits of more active
ways of relaxing.

A key word here is "rely." Relying on television for relaxation, spending as much time with it as we do, is a pattern
with serious drawbacks. However, one can make a better case
for television viewing in smaller doses. One television critic has
coined the term "mental popcorn" to describe the benefits of
limited television viewing: it does not add nutrients to the diet
but it is pleasant and harmless. There are times when all of us
simply need to stop and do nothing. Television certainly fills
that need well. The question is whether we need to do nothing
for several hours every day.

Our viewing habits demonstrate that we find television
fascinating, but when we are asked the right questions at the
right time, we discover that we are also not very happy about it.
As with other habits, we remain fascinated with television long
after much of the pleasure has gone.

One researcher who seems to have asked the right questions is
Mihaly Csikszentmihalyi, chairman of the Committee on
Human Development at the University of Chicago. He and his
colleagues recruited a group of adult volunteers to study how
they used their time and how they felt about what they were
doing. Volunteers were equipped with diaries to record their
activities for a week. They were also given beepers which were
beeped at random intervals. When the volunteers were beeped,
they were supposed to record what they were doing and how
they felt.

Csikszentmihalyi was not surprised to find that the volunteers
spent more time watching television than they did in any other
leisure activity. He *was* surprised to discover that people beeped

while viewing television tended to feel weak, passive, drowsy, lonely, unconcentrated, and unchallenged. No other activity that people engaged in made them feel so bad.

"At first," Csikszentmihalyi reported, "we didn't know if people started out watching TV feeling passive and empty hoping that TV would bring their mood up, or if it was actually the act of watching TV that brought their moods down. We went back and studied the data, and it looks like the latter is true—TV depresses their mood." Csikszentmihalyi's explanation centers around the passivity of the television experience. "Every other activity you can think of rates as a more positive experience than television, but they all take some effort and risk. Watching television is easy and safe. You can't fail. It's there for you whenever you need it. It lets you feel like you're doing something, participating, when you're really not. TV is mostly an illusion."[2] It is no wonder that something so safe and passive is a dissatisfying—even depressing—form of relaxation.

The differences between television viewing and other forms of relaxation raise the distinction between two main kinds of relaxation—active and passive. The active forms might be called recreation; the passive forms may be called rest. Television watching is a form of rest. It relaxes us not by exercising unused parts of our body or mind but simply by letting our entire body and mind shift into neutral.

The main occupant of the category "rest" is sleep. Sleep and television viewing turn out to have some interesting connections. On the average, people sleep a little less—about fifteen minutes per day—since the appearance of television than they did before. The trade-off between sleeping and viewing suggests that the two are similar activities. One researcher describes television viewing as "a stage of semisleep, inducing viewers into full sleep or into 'daydreaming.'"[3] Many people do use television as a relaxant before bedtime.

There is even a parallel between viewing and dreaming. Both involve reflections of the real world rearranged in imaginary patterns. Both repeatedly play out sexual and aggressive fantasies. We engage in both activities for a few hours out of every twenty-four, but afterward we remember very little of what we have watched or dreamed.

Perhaps the form of rest which television watching most closely resembles is daydreaming—what we do when we are staring into a fireplace or sitting alone in a restaurant waiting for dinner to be served at the end of a long day. The difference is that when we daydream we float scraps of our own memory and fancy through our consciousness, while television watching permits other people to parade the products of their imaginations through our consciousness, for their own purposes.

There is a physiological basis for comparing television watching and daydreaming. The characteristic brain-wave patterns of the brain when a person is daydreaming are dominated by what are called alpha waves. These relatively slow patterns of electrical activity on the surface of the brain indicate that the person is not processing information from the world outside himself. Erik Peper, a researcher in the field of electroencephalographic testing at San Franciso State University, describes alpha waves this way: "Alpha wave patterns . . . disappear when a person gives visual commands [focuses his eyes together on a particular object], when he takes charge of the process of seeking information. Any orienting outward to the world increases your brainwave frequencies and blocks alpha wave activity. Alpha occurs when you don't orient *to*. You sit back and have pictures in your head, but you are in a totally passive condition, unaware of the world outside of your pictures. The right phrase for alpha is really 'spaced out.' Not orienting. When a person focuses visually, or orients to anything, notices something outside himself, then she or he gets an immediate increase in faster wave activity and alpha will block [disappear]."[4]

Researchers such as Peper have discovered that even when people are watching television programs they are interested in, their brain waves indicate that they are receiving the material in this passive mode. Herbert Krugman, who has written on viewers' responses to advertising, has noted that "the basic electrical response of the brain is clearly to the medium and not to the content differences."[5]

Watching television, like daydreaming, is an alpha-wave activity. This does not mean that we are unable to absorb information, or are immune to influence when we are viewing television. We absorb certain views from television despite the uninvolved, passive, unalert way most of us view it. This is because not all learning requires concentration. As researchers such as Krugman have shown, learning of a certain sort is possible even when our minds are quite relaxed, so long as there is sufficient attention. Psychologists refer to this way of absorbing information as passive learning. Passive learning occurs when a person is neither concentrating on or putting up resistance to the source of the information. Not only can a person learn in a passive state, but suggestions made to a person when he or she is mentally relaxed are more likely to be acted on later.[6]

When we are watching television we are usually learning passively rather than actively. Our critical faculties are idle, and we are receiving a stream of images and sounds without scrutinizing them. Because our critical faculties are suspended, we are not subject to certain kinds of influence. We are not confronting issues or ideas, so we cannot be won over by an argument and brought to a radical change. But we are learning, all the same, storing up images of the world. Peper says of this, "The information goes in, but we don't react to it. It goes right into our memory pool, and perhaps we react to it later but don't know what we're reacting to."

Thus there is a paradox in the passivity of viewing the electronic screen. Television delivers a high-powered stream of informative pictures and sounds, but the medium of the information itself impairs our ability to process the information it delivers. Television greatly multiplies the number of inputs to our sight and hearing, putting us in touch with faraway people and events. But at the same time it lowers our ability to deal intelligently with the increased flow of information.

While the passivity of television viewing makes it undesirable in large quantities for adults, it may be postively harmful for children. Children's mental, physical, emotional, and spiritual development occurs as their growing bodies and minds interact with the people and things around them. Human beings progress from the passivity and dependence of infancy to the skill-mastery and autonomy of adulthood. The journey is made largely by trial and error, repetition, and experience of consequences of decisions. Mental and physical growth is an inherently active process. It cannot be poured into passive children.

We have already discussed the way that children's heavy television viewing reduces parents' opportunities to guide children's growth. However, the passivity of viewing television appears to have additional consequences for children's development. When children are spending time with television, they are withdrawn from all the normal means of growth. Television viewing deprives children of interaction with people, with things, and even, given the mental state of most viewing, with ideas. Turning on the set means turning off the process of growing up. The thousands of hours our children spend in front of the home screen may be having serious long-range effects on their development.

In a certain sense, television actually speeds up the process of growing up. Children today become familiar with adult styles, entertainment, language, sexual behavior, independence, and cynicism at an earlier age than their parents or grandparents did. But early exposure to images of the adult world is no shortcut to maturity, for in fact there are no shortcuts. Self-discipline is gained only by practice and experience—for example, the satisfaction of completing a difficult project or the guilt and shame of letting a friend down. Self-control stems, at least to a degree, from the discipline involved in acquiring skills. Character judgment comes from dealing with people. Personal relationship abilities—knowing how to handle conflicts, understanding others' needs and points of view, being appropriately

"The white hat means the guy's a virgin."

humble and assertive—come only from experience. Real adult-hood is achieved in the real world, not before the screen. Television can make children sophisticated, but not mature.

Thus television viewing is a passive form of relaxation which is less desirable than the forms of rest which it resembles. If we are to dream or daydream, surely it is usually preferable to do so ourselves, rather than immersing ourselves day after day in the dreams of other people who do not share our experience of life or perceptions of reality. Why should their expectations and fears, their longings and sorrows, become ours simply because we are too physically and mentally passive to think our own thoughts, indulge in our own reveries, or simply go to bed?

Our transformation into a society of adults and children who spend two to three or more hours a day in a largely daydreaming frame of mind has consequences. It would be surprising if television has not at least contributed to the swing away from ideals of self-discipline, thrift, and hard work, which used to characterize much of American society, to the current reigning ideals of leisure, instant gratification, and freedom from personal restrictions. Urbanization and affluence have also played a large part in this shift, but our television viewing habits have surely helped move us along. Thus television has become an agent of profound cultural change.

FOUR

Television and Our Thinking

IN 1978 GEORGE COMSTOCK of Syracuse University and several fellow researchers completed years of investigation into television's effects with the publication of a 581-page book, *Television and Human Behavior*. The authors wrote that "out of vanity, and perhaps a touch of arrogance, we have attempted to cover the entire relevant literature in English." That meant evaluating and synthesizing the findings given in more than 2,500 books, articles, reports, and other documents.[2] The preparation of the volume involved compiling bibliographies so extensive that they were published as separate books.

Of this elephantine undertaking Howard Gardner of Harvard University commented, "Although the book is a scholarly and thoughtful compendium, I read it through with a mounting sense of disappointment. Take, for example, a set of issues that has exercised the public—the effects of violent programming and of commercial messages on children. The millions of research dollars spent on these controversial issues in the last two decades seem to have yielded only two major findings, each of which might easily have been anticipated by the experimenter's proverbial grandmother." That is, children tend to imitate what they see on television—be it violent or benign—and the younger children are, the more likely they are to be taken in by the commercials. "Why do we know so little?" Gardner asked?[2]

Gardner pointed out that most television research has proceeded on lines laid down for studying the older print media.

"Why have the thousands of studies failed to tell us more about the medium of television *per se?*" he wrote. In other words, in what ways does television affect our thinking that the other media do not? Specifically, Garnder wondered, does extensive time with television, which is so visual, change people's thinking in ways that print and sound media do not?

Television's most important characteristic is its visual nature. It presents us not primarily with sounds or words but with sights. The audio portion plays a secondary role to the video. The visual portion overshadows the sound by its constant movement and change of scene. Neil Postman of New York University reported that people who were asked about what Jacob Bronowski said in the *Ascent of Man* programs "could not remember what he said, because the visual component of the shows was so dramatic."[3] One listens to radio; one watches television. Gardner's point was that we have as yet no satisfactory understanding of the consequences of the fact that television is primarily a visual, pictorial medium.

To explore this question it is necessary to reflect a little on the characteristics of pictures. Different forms of human communication are suited for conveying different aspects of reality. A caress, a song, a photograph, a dance, a personal letter—each has its own range of expression. A good-night cuddle tells a child something which no words can convey. A symphony produces an effect in the listener which he cannot adequately put into words. A documentary film gives the viewer a sense of contact with an event that any written description falls short of producing. A medical textbook provides an understanding of the body which no set of drawings could.

Christine Nystrom of New York University identifies two main differences between verbal and visual forms of communication.[4] First, language puts together its meaning-elements in sequence, while a picture presents its elements at once. Indeed, language makes sense *because* it is a commonly understood sequence of sounds forming words and words forming sentences. The order of the elements is crucial. "The dog chased the cat" is different from "The cat chased the dog" because the elements follow in a different sequence.

A picture, like a sentence, can be broken down into its separate elements—dots, lines, shades, and so forth. But these elements are not the equivalent of words. The words of a sentence can be defined in terms of other words; but the lines of a picture have no meaning apart from the particular relationship they have to each other in that particular picture. Words, sentences, and paragraphs can be translated and paraphrased into other words, but each picture is unique. So while a verbal statement can be analyzed and recommunicated in other words, a picture can only be experienced. As Nystrom puts it, "I can tell you, if you missed a lecture, what the speaker said. But I cannot tell you what you missed if you did not see 'Aristotle Contemplating the Bust of Homer' [at the Metropolitan Museum]. You had to be there."

Thus language communication is especially suitable for analysis of a situation into its parts, for logical thought that proceeds from one point to the next, for reaching rational conclusions. Pictures are especially suitable for conveying impressions, for sharing experiences.

A second difference between words and pictures is that words, by their nature, stand for other things while pictures always show particular things. The word "chalk" stands not for any specific piece of that material but for all material of that kind. However, a picture cannot show chalk in general. One must photograph a particular piece of chalk—one that is of a certain shade and length. Nystrom writes, "Language is *about* experience and, in particular, about *ideas* about experience. Pictures *are* experience. Put another way, language is reflection on experience, constructed in propositional form. Pictures are immersion in experience, reconstructed in such a way as to evoke certain feelings."

As a primarily visual medium, then, television excels at some types of communication and is weak at others. It excels in conveying a sense of what people are like, a sense of event, of excitement, power, struggle, danger, or triumph. Viewers who watched the 1980 presidential debates commented on how worrisomely intense Jimmy Carter and, even more, John Anderson seemed to be, in contrast to Ronald Reagan's aura of confidence and self-control. The candidates' personalities made a much deeper impression on many viewers than their arguments did. Viewers were interested in what the candidates said, of course. But they particularly wanted to see *how* Carter, Anderson, and Reagan were going to say it—how they were going to handle themselves in a public, high-pressure confrontation.

Other examples come readily to mind of ways in which television, intending to inform, makes a greater impression on our feelings than our intellect. From a documentary on endangered wilderness areas, one recalls a vivid picture of bulldozers brutally shearing away topsoil and wildflowers. The lasting impression of a documentary on gay liberation is of one gay leader's thin-lipped, belligerent determination to achieve social acceptance for homosexual life styles.

Television is unsurpassed at this sort of thing. It satisfies our desire to know what the person is like, to be there, to see for ourselves. To point out television's strength in this kind of communication is not to criticize it. We can better deal with the world if we have somehow experienced our fellow inhabitants as real human beings, not merely as advocates of ideas or symbols of movements. The point is simply to underline an aspect of television's essence: When we are viewing television we are *having the experience* of seeing what is actually far away. The experience is the key. We are dealing with a medium which is not strong at communicating abstract ideas in logical arrangements.

Television is also structured in ways that are not conducive to logical thought. As Christine Nystrom points out, television tends to compress experience by quick editing and program formats that tend to reduce complex problems to simple solutions. This is true of many news and documentary programs as well as fictional entertainment. Television rearranges experience by breaking it up into brief snatches that are then fitted together in patterns designed to heighten excitement rather than reveal the logical relationships between causes and effects.

The differences between verbal and visual ways of communicating are not absolute, of course. Words are often used in dramatic, emotion arousing ways. Pictorial presentations, whether in magazine photo journalism or television documentaries, can be assembled with rigorous logic and a grasp of complexities. Indeed, television, like magazines, newspapers, movies, and many books, is a combination of words and pictures. Because it is visual, television tends to focus on material that appeals to the emotions, to organize its content in dramatic, exciting, episodic ways, to simplify. Because it uses words, it also has plot and story, logical analysis, and some appreciation of complexities. The point is that television is primarily a visual medium, and its tendencies are stronger in the first rather than the second direction.

Television's pictorial qualities have serious implications. Consider the fact that television is most people's main source of news. Even many people who read newspapers and magazines regard television as their main informant about current events. For our knowledge and understanding of political and economic happenings, we are relying on a medium which brings certain strengths and weaknesses to the task. Television can give us powerful impressions of events and people, but it is less suited to conveying information in ways that foster analytical thinking, thinking that compares what is seen with individual experience, thinking that organizes knowledge into causes and effects.

Columnist and political philosopher George Will has remarked on television's weakness at in-depth communication: "Television is a slave to an inherently superficial newsgathering instrument—the camera. TV exists to present vivid portrayal, but much of the world simply cannot be captured on film. For example, you cannot take a picture of the law of supply and demand. That is one reason why television has had trouble figuring out how to use its technology to cover economic news."

Will finds fault with the quick pace of television news—the organization of material into exciting segments, cutting rapidly from scene to scene, topic to topic. He notes that there is a trend toward assuming "that any argument about public policy can be presented in 30 seconds. . . . Because of the pace and speed of journalism (which reflects the pace and speed of modern life, particularly on television) there is a tendency to simplify problems. Problems are often presented as at most two-sided, when in fact there are usually a dozen or so sides to every issue."[5]

An example of television's tendency to simplify is its focus on individuals. As Will points out, television must show pictures, but economic dynamics are hard to picture, as are social classes, political philosophies, and alliances of interest groups. Television consequently zeroes in on the individual men and women who are involved. People, of course, can be seen through a camera lens. Underlying causes and long-range implications receive inadequate treatment as the camera is aimed chiefly at the struggle of leading individuals.

We must question our major reliance on television for news in view of television's predominantly visual character and the passive state we are usually in when we watch it. No perfect alternatives present themselves. Newspapers and magazines have their faults too. They often oversimplify, seek out the merely dramatic, focus on personalities, and so on, as television does. They do so partly to compete with television. However, the print media offer a wider selection of informative and analytical material than the evening news, which often amounts to little more than a headline service.

In practice, we give the print media second place in our news-seeking merely because they require more mental effort than watching television. A more reasonable approach would be to consider what might be the most judicious mix of televised and printed information. At present, television, being easier, wins out. The result is that we are a society whose degree of in-touchness exceeds our degree of genuine understanding.

Turning to children, the pictorial nature of television raises a basic developmental issue. The issue is: What effect does immersion in a primarily visual form of communication have on children's minds? We have already found that television viewing, by taking children away from reading, conversation, and so on, has an indirect negative effect on children's progress in reading. But what are the *direct* effects of television on children's intellectual growth? How does viewing affect mental development?

Neil Postman, whose research we have already mentioned (people who saw a television documentary remembered the pictures but forgot the words) speaks for many educators when he asserts that children's attention spans are shrinking and that they have rising expectations for a high degree of stimulation in the classroom. Many educators contend that television lies behind these changes. It is close to impossible to prove such a contention, but the frequency with which educators voice it merits serious attention for the claim.

Postman says: "Schools assume that there are some things you must know before you can learn other things. They assume that not all things are as immediately accessible as they are on television and that it takes hard work and lengthy periods of study to attain many desirable things, such as knowledge, that are not immediately visible. Yet because the attention span of children is contracting, teachers are under terrific pressure to make everything relevant. . . . The temptation is very great for teachers to substitute for real learning something that's fairly jazzy and that will immediately capture the attention of the kids."[6] Here we see again the effects of television's visual structure—the rapid-fire succession of images that flash before the viewer, offering visual and emotional stimulation while he is in a state of mental passivity.

Postman also scores the effects of television's basic visual orientation. "A high degree of visual stimulation . . . tends to distract attention away from language. . . . Although human speech is heard on television, it is the picture that always contains the most important meanings. Television can never teach what a medium like a book can teach, and yet educators are always trying to pretend that they can use television to

promote cognitive habits and the intellectual discipline that
print promotes. In this respect they will always be doomed to
failure. Television is not a suitable medium for conveying ideas,
because an idea is essentially language—words and sentences."

A declining ability for concentrated, complex, abstract
thought, which Postman finds on elementary and high school
levels, is also a source of concern to educators on the college
level. Michael Novak compares television's quick cutting
between two or three simultaneous threads of a story with
students' willingness to have several lines of argument
developed at the same time. Conceding that there may be
advantages to such a readiness to juggle several thoughts at
once, Novak thinks that such habits of thought conflict with
more disciplined mental processes which are necessary in every
branch of learning.

"The systems of teaching which I learned in my student
days—careful and exact exegesis proceeding serially from point
to point, the careful definition and elucidation of terms in an
argument, and the careful scrutiny of chains of inference, and
the like—now meet new forms of resistance. There has always
been resistance to mental discipline. One has only to read the
notebooks of students from medieval universities to recognize
this well-established tradition of resistance. But today the
minds and affections of the brighter students are teeming with
images, vicarious experiences, and indeed actual travel and
accomplishments. Their minds race ahead and around the
flanks of lines of argument."[7]

Relatively little research has focused on the mental effects of
television's pictorial nature and structures—which is what
Howard Gardner complained of in response to Comstock's
exhaustive survey of findings. But the studies that have been
done tend to confirm the conclusions of Postman and Novak
that television affects children's mental development.

On the plus side, television seems to stimulate the development of visual and spatial abilities. For example, it has been
reported that television helps children who have difficulty

picking out significant details in larger scenes. Apparently television's use of zoom, which narrows the view from a wide picture to a single detail, trains children's eyes to do the same. It has also been found that specially designed television material for children, used on programs like *Sesame Street*, can train children to scan from left to right. This is a reading readiness skill which some children develop only with difficulty. (Of course, almost no television programs *do* develop this skill.)

On the minus side are the results of a study by researchers at Harvard Project Zero. Laurene Meringoff and her colleagues divided children into two groups. One was shown an animated version of a story on television, while the other had the story read to them while they watched the book's still-picture illustrations on a television. The two versions of the story were equal in length and as close in content as could be designed.

The children who watched the animated story were less able to remember the story or answer questions about it than the children who had the reading-illustration version. The animated-story children were also less skilled at repeating just what they had heard. When they were asked to explain certain details, they were more inclined to rely on visual cues rather than inferences from the story and their own experience. For example, all the children agreed that it had been difficult for a story character to wield a certain object. But the animated story children drew their conclusions from the expression on the character's face, while those who heard the story drew their conclusions from their real-life experience with the object. The animated-story group estimated time and distance in the story on the basis of how times and distances appeared in the cartoon; the other group gave more plausible, real-life estimates.[8]

Children who had the story read to them were thus more active in exercising mental faculties such as plot memorization, dialogue recall, and comparison of story events with similar real-life events. These are the kinds of mental processes associated with language. The children who saw the story in cartoon form on television, by contrast, had an experience that

"*It's shows like this that make me wish I could read,*"

was more immediate (less clearly connected with plot), were geared to visual cues rather than dialogue, and were less able to compare one set of events with another.

Meringoff's study gives experimental support to the view that immersion in television is changing the way people growing up in our society perceive the world and reason about it. Gardner writes: "Exposure to television apparently highlights a different line of inference than experience with books. Thus, the child who views many hours of television, day after day, may well develop different kinds of imaginative powers, or, as McLuhan might claim, a different 'ratio among imaginations,' from one weaned on books. . . . The temporal and spatial outlooks of the TV freak and the bookworm may differ in fundamental respects."[9]

Is this a desirable situation? Should we greet with approval the rise of a generation of people who perceive and conceptualize the world differently, a generation with new habits of thought?

It is impossible to give a complete answer to the question, because we are still very far from understanding the phenomenon. If watching television gives people an eye for significant details, if it trains people to move rapidly from one scene to another and one idea to another without confusion, then something has been gained. However, if heavy involvement with the visual medium slows growth in language-related abilities, then we have cause for concern. Are we willing to see the enlargement of our children's visual and spacial perceptions if it means their ability to marshall ideas clearly and logically will be underdeveloped?

Our crowded, complicated world is going to need more people with acutely developed language-related skills. Rapidly developing technologies call for men and women who have developed their ability to proceed mentally from the specific case to the general rule, who can comprehend the relationships between the parts of a whole, who can remember large amounts of information. Men and women with such basic skills are needed to staff our hospitals, plan our cities, head our corporations, and keep the whole complex apparatus of modern society functioning. Social and political changes will continue to create the need for citizens who are able to understand complex issues and can distinguish well-conceived from ill-conceived proposals. And if society as a whole will need increasing numbers of people whose minds are trained to deal with complexities, certainly the church will be in even more urgent need of them. The church around the world today confronts both vast opportunities for the gospel and profound challenges.

The preceding chapter presented evidence that television has played an indirect role in the declining levels of scholastic achievement of successive high school classes since the 1960s. The explanation was that television viewing subtracts time from activities which contribute to intellectual growth, especially reading and conversation with adults. The evidence regarding television's *direct* effects on children's thinking suggests that it impedes their development of mental habits which they most need if they are to grow into useful citizens, mature human beings, and effective servants of God.

Television challenges the very process of education. The words "to educate" come from the Latin term which means "to lead forth," or "to lead out of." Education leads out of a state of not being able to do or understand. Western education has always been directed toward leading the individual into an ability to read, write, and carry on the mental processes that accompany language. The task of Western education has always been *toward* rather than *away from* language and the kinds of thinking it allows. By contrast, despite its apparent success at conveying information, television's hidden curriculum slows individuals' progress toward mastery of language and language-related abilities.

Children's growth toward these mental abilities occurs according to internally timed mechanisms as well as outside training. Children below the age of six, for instance, respond to the immediate, concrete situation they happen to be in. Their mental equipment has not matured enough to enable them to consider present events in terms of larger units of time. They are limited in their ability to see present actions in light of future consequences. Children younger than about the age of fourteen are incapable of certain kinds of abstraction—going from the concrete detail to the general principle or category. Thus there is a natural development from the baby's mental processes, which are carried out entirely without language, to the adult's thinking, which through language is able to see beyond the immediate and specific to grasp the principle and rule. Only by the adult's thinking are we able to master the environment.

Seen against this natural developmental background, children's immersion in the visual medium of television appears as a drag on the natural course of development. Television promotes modes of thinking which children are normally outgrowing. Unlike formal education, which attempts to harness the dynamics of natural development and guide them to the realization of their potential, television provides opportunities for the child to engage in immature thinking. Seated before the screen, he or she may respond to concrete details rather than trying to fit things together mentally. Viewing is a time of emotional rather than intellectual response, of passive stimulation rather than an experience of mental stretching to memorize, imagine, or understand. Seated before the television, the child has pulled off into a rest area along the freeway of mental growth.

Thus, while providing us with an increasing volume of information, television to some degree erodes our ability to think about it coherently. For contact with the world we are relying ever more heavily on a medium which tends to undermine our ability to develop intellectual control. Surely this is one of the more remarkable paradoxes of contemporary life.

Television watching is a peculiarly passive experience, and television communicates mainly in pictures rather than words. We may draw a simple concluion: we ought to deal with television with a fair degree of caution. These are significant dynamics. They are not well understood. They do not warrant the view that heavy, regular immersion in television is healthy and beneficial. Rather they justify a reconsideration of our viewing habits.

FIVE

A Curious Access
to Our Minds

WHEN WE WATCH TELEVISION, we are seeing life happening through someone else's eyes. Because we have become accustomed to it, we rarely consider that the ability to do this is something entirely new in history. Before the development of motion pictures around the turn of the century, no one ever saw anything *happening* through anyone else's eyes. From the cave painters of long ago who filled their walls with herds of gracefully bounding antelope, to the engravers of nineteenth-century newspapers who offered morning readers scenes of the most recent battle, men and women could only show what they *had* seen. No one could ever show someone else what they *were seeing*. Poets, storytellers, and journalists could describe; listeners and readers could mentally re-create the scenes in their minds. Painters and sculptors could make representations. Photographers could even record what they had actually seen for an instant. But it was not until motion pictures and television that people could communicate the experience of seeing the moving world *as they were seeing it*.

Despite a great deal of study and research by scholars and by professionals in the motion picture and television industries, we still do not understand the consequences of our newly developed ability. Much has been written about the educational uses of television, the cultural effects of the information and values it communicates, its power—or powerlessness—to influence people's decisions to buy particular products or vote for particular candidates. But the very act of viewing television has not been thoroughly understood.

Television viewing—seeing through someone else's eyes—is a complex activity. When we look at a painting or photograph of a person or thing, we are always fairly conscious that we are looking at an image of the person rather than the person himself. We are conscious that we are looking at pictures. For example, tourists who travel to Assisi, Italy, and look at the portrait of Francis there are aware that it is only a painting. "This is the only painting which may be an actual likeness of Francis," they comment. "How well-preserved it is." Similarly, when a friend shows us snapshots of her vacation, we remark not only on her vacation but on her photography. As we shuffle through the photos we might ask her what kind of film she used or note what a beautiful picture a particular one is. But when we pull the television switch to on, and people speak and police cars whiz down the street, our awareness that we are looking at pictures recedes, and it is as though we are actually seeing people and events.

This is evident from the way we talk. We say we saw the President on TV last night, not that we saw pictures of him. We say that we are "watching the Olympic skiing competition"—as though we are witnesses—not that we are "seeing the program about the skiing"—which would indicate a sense of distance from the event. We know we are not there, but we speak as though we were.

When television began, this phenomenon was a source of amazement. And through the years events have occasionally refreshed our sense of wonder at television's ability to make distant things seem present. Many of us who saw Jack Ruby gun down Lee Harvey Oswald on a Sunday morning or saw the American astronauts walking on the moon can recall exactly where we were when they saw these events on live television. We were impressed with the extraordinariness of the transaction that was taking place. We who were in conversation on our way out to church were suddenly present at a murder in Dallas. We who were in the middle of cooking dinner became present at a stroll across the surface of the moon.

Most of the time, however, our sense of the extraordinary fades into the background of our minds. Even in 1946 an early observer could write, "The wonder of television passes quickly." We simply accept the fact that when we watch television we seem to be seeing people and events which, for the most part, we are unlikely ever to meet in person or witness during our whole lives.

What are we actually seeing? What our *eyes* are focusing on are patterns of light and color formed by electron streams on the inner surface of a cathode ray tube. But our *minds* are seeing the actual persons and events being televised. As William Fore has put it, television makes "a whole world seem real to us when it is in fact nothing more than bright phosphors dancing on a piece of glass." Seeing only a lighted screen, we think we are watching people and things. More precisely, while *knowing* we are seeing only a lighted screen, we have an experience which we can only describe as watching people and things. Television thus accomplishes one of mankind's long-standing ambitions. It also performs a feat of illusion which every magician in history might envy.

The fact that we have the experience of doing something which we know rationally we are not raises the possibility that television's effects on our minds may be different from what we might think. Take, for example, a dramatic program about a gutsy, iconoclastic surgeon at a large metropolitan hospital (an idea which Hollywood recycles every few years). We know that the man we are seeing is an actor playing in a fictional story and that at least some of what we see in the program misrepresents how things happen in a surgeon's professional life. But the program is realistic rather than fantastic. The people are appropriately dressed for their roles as doctors, nurses, and patients. The medical equipment looks genuine. The characters' jargon has the ring of authenticity. We know that we are seeing actors in a studio somewhere near Los Angeles. But do we therefore regard it all as illusory and unreliable?

Not entirely. Intriguing pieces of evidence suggest that when our eyes are on the television something more is going on than meets the eye. Consider these items. In the first five years of the program *Marcus Welby, M.D.*, the program received more than a quarter of a million letters from viewers, most containing requests for medical advice. More than once, lawyers and clients have used material from television programs in the courtroom. On one occasion an attorney objected to the manner in which the prosecutor was speaking to the witness. "I know," the judge replied. "I've watched Perry Mason too, but that's not a valid objection in a court of law."

What is going on here? Did some people actually believe that Welby was a physician, Mason a counselor at law? Apparently while viewers know that they are watching fiction, some of them are so impressed with the seeming reality of it that they begin to relate to it as real. Television, it seems, has a curious access to our minds, an ability to bypass to some degree our rational evaluation of material as fictional or distorted.

Two researchers at the University of Pennsylvania, George Gerbner and Larry Gross, write:

Anecdotes and examples should not trivialize the real point, which is that even the most sophisticated can find many important components of their knowledge of the real world derived wholly or in part from fictional representation. The dominant stylistic convention of Western narrative art— novel, plays, films, TV drama—is that of representational realism. However contrived television plots are, viewers assume that they take place against a backdrop of the real world. Nothing impeaches the basic "reality" of the world of television drama. It is also highly informative. That is, it offers to the unsuspecting viewers a continuous stream of "facts" and impressions about the way of the world, about the constancies and vagaries of human nature, and about the consequences of actions. . . .

A normal adult viewer is not unaware of the fictiveness of television drama. No one calls the police or an ambulance when a character in a television program is shot. "War of the Worlds"—type scares are rare, if they occur at all. Granting this basic awareness on the part of the viewers, one may still wonder how often and to what degree all viewers suspend their disbelief in the reality of the symbolic world.[1]

We may indeed wonder. Gerbner and Gross identify one factor which makes television—even its fictional entertainment offerings—"highly informative." This is viewers' assumption that while the stories are "made up" they take place in the real world. A second factor is viewers' lack of familiarity with the slices of the world which are portrayed. Most of us, for instance, have only a slight acquaintance with surgical suites, doctors' conference rooms, and medical procedures. Television programs fill in the blanks in our knowledge. Of course, neither of these factors is unique to television. When we read a novel about doctors and hospitals, most of us assume that the background is realistic and the story supplies us with information about the field of medicine that we did not know before. The unique factor that comes into play when we watch television, however, is that with television we have the experience of seeing it all happen.

Seeing, like the other senses, puts us in contact with the world. If we are in immediate sense contact with something, we know it is there. We may have questions about it, but we are sure that it is real. For example, if you tell me a story, I know that you are speaking to me, even though I may have my doubts about what you are telling me. If you draw a picture for me, I am certain the picture is really there, although I may not be convinced that your drawing is accurate. If I watch a CBS program about a gutsy surgeon, I know he is really there, although I may also know that he is not really a doctor.

The technology around us has changed; television now extends the reach of our senses of sight and hearing far beyond their natural range. At the same time, the psychological mechanisms by which we perceive the world have not changed at all. Our minds are put together the same way that humans' minds have always been put together. Our mental structures are the same: we are programmed to believe our senses. We know what the world is like through what we see and hear, just as our grandparents and great-grandparents did. We believe our eyes and ears the same way all our ancestors did. We believe what we see simply because we are seeing it.

However, while what we are seeing on television is *real*—real human beings and objects—it is not always *true*. We are not seeing a true-to-life, balanced view of how the world actually is. Nevertheless, our seeing-is-believing mechanism goes right on working as before. Of course, one part of our mind knows that the story is fiction or that the newscasts and documentaries are a rigorously selective portion of the facts. But anyone who thinks that we therefore discount the reality of it might contemplate the quarter of a million letters to that noted physician, Marcus Welby. Once again the paradox is this: television vastly extends the range of our sense but in a way that impedes or bypasses our ability to rationally and actively deal with the input. The medium engages our basic contact-with-reality mechanisms, that is, our senses, in a way that bypasses rational judgment.

Another way of stating the paradox is to say that with television we have both the advantages and disadvantages of seeing the world through other people's eyes. To see the world through someone else's eyes means more than borrowing a pair of eyeballs. The guard who sits in the control room of a parking structure watching the coming and going of cars and pedestrians on television monitors has merely added some electronic eyes. But if we watch anything more interesting on television than parked cars and exit ramps, we are doing more than looking out at the world through other people's eyes. We are seeing the world through their minds. The choice of subject matter, the way the subject will be dealt with, what will be shown and what will be excluded, what will be treated as important and what ignored—these are decisions that the writer, director, cameraman, and producer have made. The program which results shows us life happening from their point of view. This is as true

of documentary programs as of entertainment offerings.

We ought to consider carefully the benefits and costs of seeing the world through other's eyes. On the one hand, something happens which every artist has sought to do—a sharing of his or her point of view. What every journalist aspires to do—to show things as they actually are—television in a sense does. On the other hand the medium gives us not primarily ideas or explanations that we can agree or disagree with, but sights and sounds which our senses receive simply as real. What we *see happening* shapes our view of the world—what it is like, how its parts and participants are put together and function. So looking at the world through other people's eyes means submitting to them a basic means by which we orient ourselves to the world.

The term "submitting" is appropriate. We are submitting our minds to someone else's. There is an irony here. We treasure our freedom. Perhaps more than any society in the past we are sensitive to the dangers of methods or styles of government and education which curb individuals' freedom to form their own convictions. It is curious, then, that we spend hours every day submitting our minds to others' minds. A more intimate and questionable form of submission could not be imagined.

This aspect of television, like all others, is a matter of special concern regarding children. Television's effects on adults must overcome the attitudes, experience, and knowledge accumulated during a lifetime. Children are more malleable.

The notion that our children are spending a great deal of time seeing the world through others' minds has troubling implications for parents, especially Christian parents. Christians recognize a responsibility not only to provide materially for their children and equip them for success in their careers and personal relationships but even more to train them in faith and love of God. Christian parents want to see their children reach adulthood with a Christian understanding of reality, with their minds formed according to God's revelation of himself. Allowing children to ingest the non-Christian worldview of television hardly supports this growth.

Indeed, television gives us much to be uneasy about. Television viewing is a puzzling and paradoxical behavior. For two to three or more hours a day, for 50,000 to 75,000 or more hours of an average person's life, we are watching television. For this whole time we are seeing the world through other people's eyes and other people's minds. What the long-range social effects of this situation may be no one can say for sure. But we can safely make two points: (1) this situation is entirely without precedent in human history. We cannot predict its consequences by looking at the experience of any other society or age, because it is unique. In no other society has almost everyone spent five to eight whole years of their lives looking at the world through others' eyes. And (2) it is unreasonable to think that this situation will not have a deep effect on us as individuals and as a society. A society in which everyone gives a few selected views of reality extensive access to their minds from cradle to grave—what could more reasonably be expected to produce a profoundly different society of people than that?

In the following chapters we will look at some of the dynamics by which television, with its curious access to our minds, affects our thinking, and we will look at the clash between the views and values of secular television programming and the outlook we should be developing as Christians. But first, a note about research into television's effects.

If people imitate what they see on television, Russell Baker asks, why aren't gas station attendants more pleasant? "I have been watching gas-station workmen [on television] for 25 years, and such a splendid bunch of working men I never expect to meet. They smile when it is pouring rain and a motorist asks them to check his tire pressure. They explain tie rods and carburetor sludge with a lucidity that clarifies all, and not only explain, but also do something about them." The television model of beaming gas station attendants, seen in hundreds of oil company commercials, is flawless. "If television really provided the models whose behavior we copy," Baker reasons, "filling-station men would be the sweetest, kindest, warmest, swellest guys on this wonderful old earth of ours." In fact, however, they are no more or less eager to serve than most folks who have a grimy and often tiresome job to do. "When," Baker asks, "was the last time you drove into a real filling station in a pouring rain, asked the gas pumper to check your tires, and received a smile?" The smiling example of countless cheerful television models runs aground on the hard realities of everyday life.[2]

It is a mistake, George Will writes, to exaggerate television's influence. "To represent situation-comedy shows as shapers of the nation's consciousness is to portray the public as more passive and plastic than it is." In Will's view, for instance, it is silly to claim that television made the civil rights movement of the sixties. "The movement had on its side great leaders, centuries of grievances, the Constitution, and justice. It benefited from television, but did not depend upon it." Neither did television unmake Lyndon Johnson, as some have alleged. "Disintegration at home and defeat abroad" did that. "Journalists, and perhaps even serious scholars," Will writes, "are prone to believe that [television] turns the world. But the world is not that easy to turn."[3]

"Common sense," Dennis Meredith argues, "tells us that we humans are not really television zombies, electronically lobotomized and trained to buy whatever is advertised. Nor are we really gulled by the warped worldview television presents, but are fully capable of comparing the real world and sorting out the medium's fantasies and biases, as well as its failures."[4]

The common note in Baker's, Will's, and Meredith's disclaimers regarding television's impact is an appeal to common sense. What we see on the screen may have some effects on us, but television certainly has not persuaded us to follow all its models, accept whatever political views it presents, or obediently buy all the products it advertises. We have all watched a fair amount of television, and few if any of us would admit to being turned into robots or being otherwise mentally taken over.

The issue regarding television's content, then, does not have to do with extreme or bizarre patterns of influence or control. The issue has to do with more subtle influences which mingle with many other real-life factors. Loosening ties to neighborhood and family, changing ideals in the field of education, shifting opinions among intellectual leaders at universities and seminaries, economic and technological developments—all these and more feed into the processes influencing our opinions and behavior. The part that television plays is very difficult to sort out. Certainly it would be simplistic to attribute any major change in people's thinking and behavior solely to television.

The presence of many other influences on our thinking and

behavior is not the only reason we have difficulty in determining the effects of television's program content. There is also the long-term nature of television's influence. How is it possible to measure the effects of thousands of hours of viewing by a person or an entire society over a period of twenty or thirty years? One researcher notes that "experiments are well-suited to the study of explosions—sudden and dramatic events with predictably sudden effects. But experiments are inefficient for the study of slow cultivation, erosion, and corrosion."[5] Doctors face a similar problem when they study the effects of food additives, air pollution, and habitual inactivity. However, doctors at least have animals whose laboratory responses may shed light in the effects on humans. For television studies, there are no laboratory animals. Neither are there "controls," that is, people who do not watch any television and therefore provide a control against which to compare findings regarding those who watch. We all watch.

Various studies do, however, indicate the effects of television's content on our lives. Some of these studies have followed the same group of people for several years. Some have compared light viewers with heavy viewers. Some have demonstrated short-term changes which television causes in controlled laboratory situations. Some have proceeded in other ways. No one fully understands the dynamics by which television affects people's thinking and behavior. Several dynamics seem to be involved, almost always in combination with one another. We will examine three in the next chapter.

SIX

Arousal, Role Models, and Behavior Modification

T HE FIRST DYNAMIC of television content's influence is the simplest. What we see on television arouses us. It stimulates states of mind and feelings and thus, ultimately, it affects our thinking and behavior. The mental passivity that accompanies much of our television viewing does not mean we are unreceptive to stimuli. Rather it means that our critical faculties are relaxed. Our minds are not available for demanding intellectual activity. But we are open to stimulation on various levels, especially basic ones such as feelings of fear, excitement, anger, sexual arousal, and other desires.

The years of research during television's first age have shown clearly that television heightens viewers' aggressive mood and leads to more aggressive behavior. In the early 1970s an advisory committee to the surgeon general on television and social behavior concluded that children who grow up watching large amounts of violence are more aggressive not only in childhood but also later in life. F. Scott Andison, a sociologist at the University of Victoria, British Columbia, surveyed all the major studies of the connection between television violence and viewer aggressiveness between 1956 and 1976. He wrote, "We can conclude on the basis of the present data cumulation that television . . . probably does stimulate a higher amount of aggression in individuals within society."[1]

Studies indicate that television not only desensitizes viewers to violence and lowers their threshhold for expressing violence, but that it also directly raises viewers' levels of aggressiveness. One study which supports this view was conducted by David Loye of the U.C.L.A. School of Medicine. Using male subjects in their homes, Loye investigated the effects of televised violence on both behavior and mood. He measured viewers' mood by giving them various psychological tests immediately after they watched the violent programming. Loye compared these men with those who watched programs showing people helping each other in various ways. The second group did not show an increase in helpful kinds of behavior at home, but they did evidence a decline in aggressive mood, and they were less angry, impatient, and ornery with their families, as reported by their wives. The first group—the violence viewers—showed a heightened aggressive mood and more hurtful behavior.[2]

Verifying the link between television violence and viewer aggressiveness has been a preoccupation of professionals studying the medium. This research has been complicated by researchers' use of different definitions of aggressiveness in different studies. Some have defined aggressiveness as violent criminal behavior; for others, aggressiveness is any behavior that harms another, whether in word or deed. Watching a lot of televised violence has been shown to contribute to both kinds of aggressiveness. However, the rather loose, blanket condemnation of all aggressiveness that pervades much criticism of television violence is open to question.

Criminal violence and other harmful expressions of aggressiveness are undesirable and un-Christian, but other expressions of aggressiveness are beneficial. For example, we want the police to be aggressive in their investigation of crime. Many Americans wish church leaders in the 1940s and 1950s had tried more aggressively to overcome racism within and outside the churches.

"Aggressive" has two common meanings. It means a combative readiness and disposition to dominate. It also means a driving, forceful energy, enterprise, and initiative. The problem with some of the research and discussions of television's stimulation of aggressiveness is a failure to think clearly about what kind of aggressiveness is being considered undesirable—criminal aggressiveness? any harmful aggressiveness? all aggressiveness?

Some critics seem to believe that all aggressiveness is to be shunned. For example, Richard Dienstbier, a psychologist at the University of Nebraska, wrote this about the effects of television:

> The expression of tendencies toward aggression and violence must be controlled; it is difficult to think of examples of positive uses of violence. An increased capacity to enjoy, express, and communicate our aggression would not appear to further the well-being of humanity, especially when these activities are considered on an international scale.[8]

Dienstbier believes that sexual desires are inherently good and aggressiveness is inherently bad. Therefore, he says, television should be free to present sexually arousing material but not material that stimulates aggressiveness. The personality ideal in the background here is that of the sexually liberated man or woman who is always nice to everyone.

A more balanced and realistic position would be that both sexuality and aggressiveness are God-given, naturally good dynamics. Sexuality enables men and women to form families and have children. Aggressiveness enables them to take the initiative, to act decisively, to overcome obstacles, to persevere, to withstand opposition, to fight when necessary. However, in fallen human society neither sexuality nor aggressiveness functions as God intended. Both must be directed toward righteousness with the power of the Holy Spirit.

Christians should distinguish their critique of television's aggression-stimulating properties from secular critiques such as Dienstbier's. A basic aggressiveness, formed according to principles of righteousness, is an important quality of Christian character. Zeal is a scriptural term which is close in meaning for appropriately directed aggressiveness. Thus, while Christians, along with many others, will find much television violence undesirable, they may not deplore aggressiveness as much as some other critics do. The Christian goal is not to eradicate aggressiveness but to express it in ways that build up rather than tear down.

To no one's surprise, sexually explicit material on television has been shown to be sexually arousing. Broadcast television has been much quicker to present sexual innuendo than to depict sexual activity, but it has moved toward more explicit sex, and cable television has moved much farther. Psychologists disagree about whether and what kinds of sexual material is *harmful*, not whether the material is *arousing*. Those who take the position that it is not harmful do so because (1) the evidence collected so far shows that people who have committed sexual crimes have generally seen *less* sexually explicit material than most people have, and (2) they believe that the arousing material causes a build-up of sexual desire which can be safely discharged through "sexual relations with a regular partner, or through masturbation."[4] Dienstbier, who holds this view, expresses the perspective of many sex educators when he advocates free access for adolescents and adults to explicit sexual material. In other words, he wants what most people would term pornography to be available in the media and in sex education courses in the schools. Psychologists such as Dienstbier argue that erotic material reduces sexual deviancy by teaching viewers the appropriate ways to discharge sexual tensions.

With the appearance of cable channels specializing in what is sometimes called soft porn, Dienstbier and his colleagues may have their wish. But in fact, psychologists such as Dienstbier take a view of sexual desires and behavior which is completely contrary to the Christian view. What is instructive here is that all professional observers, whatever their moral values, recognize that televised sexual material is arousing. The disagreement over sexual material regards the desirability of the consequences.

The last body of evidence that television arouses us hardly needs lengthy discussion. The most carefully crafted and expensive pieces of television content are based on the belief that television can arouse desires: commercials. However they work, they are certainly intended to make viewers want what they see. Commercials may not directly alter our beliefs about products or our attitudes toward them. The formation of beliefs and attitudes requires a higher level of active conscious involvement than that which takes place in most viewing of television. What commercials do is speak a very basic language—the language of images and desires. Commercials position products in our minds as desirable in connection with some physical or social need we feel. When we are later in the market for the item, we are more likely to choose one we are familiar with and which has these desirable associations.

The most substantial demonstration that commercials succeed in initiating this sequence is the very existence of the massive structure of commercial television. From the three major networks to the smallest local station, the entire structure rests on the willingness of businessmen to pay billions of dollars to put their ads on the screen. Commercial television is commercial in two senses: it is founded on this income from the world of commerce, and, more precisely, it is founded on commercials. The stimulation of desires in millions of hearts in thirty-second segments—that is what television is really all about.

As Gaye Tuchman, sociologist of Queens College in New York, has pointed out, in the television business, the customers are not the viewers, despite the networks' rhetoric to that effect. The real clients are the corporations which put down the cash in order to have the opportunity to stimulate desires. The product being sold is not the programs but the viewers themselves; the networks are selling such-and-such a number of eyeballs lined up before the screen for such-and-such a price per thousand. The programs, far from being the product, are the marketable industrial byproduct of the manufacturing process used to create the product, which is the viewers themselves. Fundamentally, commercial television is not about the entertaining of minds but about the arousing of desires.[5]

Jenny Mitchell, age 12, likes to watch a dramatic program on Tuesday nights about a group of American espionage agents operating in Central America. The leader of the spies is an attractive, clever, self-reliant young woman named Carole Walker. Watching Ms. Walker, Jenny is getting interested in knowing how to defend herself, working for the government when she grows up, and traveling alone to other places in the world.

It is only common sense to think that people imitate what they see on television. But it is helpful to know that numerous empirical studies support this supposition; as one researcher has remarked, it was by common sense that people used to think that the world is flat. Empirical studies also shed light on how the modeling process works. Almost all the evidence comes from studies of children. This represents the assumption by researchers that children are more likely than adults to model themselves on television characters. More research needs to be done on adult modeling of television behavior, but there is no reason to think that adults are not influenced by video models also, even if less so than children.

Researchers have discovered that children tend to imitate not only live models but also filmed adults and even cartoon characters, although it seems that the effects of live models are more enduring.[6] If viewers think what they are seeing is real rather than fictional, they are more likely to model themselves on it. For example, children who were told that a film portraying conflict and rioting was news coverage showed more aggressive behavior afterwards than those who believed the film was part of a Hollywood movie.[7]

If realism enhances the effectiveness of television models, then dramatic programs which consciously strive for realism may be especially influential. Soap operas, for instance, deliberately employ techniques which strengthen the impression that they are slices from the lives of real people. Some researchers at the University of Massachusetts have pointed out that "the perceived reality of soap opera content is accounted for partly by formal features of language, such as hesitation phenomena—false starts, repetitions, filled pauses, and unfilled pauses."[8] This mimicking of real life, we may conclude, raises the degree to which soap opera characters will be taken as models by the women and men who view them.

People seem to more readily imitate models who function in situations which are similar to their own. For example, children are more likely to imitate televised violent behavior which takes place in circumstances that resemble their own, such as neighborhood or classroom.[9] One reason may be that video portrayals which touch close to home make a greater impact on our minds. Another reason may be that the portrayal includes cues for certain kinds of behavior. When we encounter those cues in our own lives, there is some tendency to respond in a way that imitates what we have seen. For instance, children shown violent behavior against a person with a certain name are more likely to act violently when they are afterwards exposed to someone with that name than when they are exposed to someone with a different name.

People are also more likely to model themselves on characters who are rewarded for their behavior. Models who are successful in gaining power, prestige, or other rewards for behavior are more influential than those who do not. Television characters who act in clearly deviant ways, such as violent criminals, are usually punished. But many television models of less obvious kinds of wrongdoing and wrong values do in fact seem to benefit from their actions. People also seem to be more likely to model themselves on members of their own sex.[10]

All in all, considering the realistic texture of the Carole Walker series, her success in and enjoyment of her work, and her being a woman, it is not surprising that Jenny Mitchell is impressed. Based on what is known of the dynamics of modeling and television, we may expect that when Jenny gets old enough to enter adult situations reminiscent of Carole

Walker's world, Ms. Walker's presence will be one of the influences that affect Jenny's attitudes and decisions.

In recent years, research into the modeling dynamics of television has shifted from study of violent behavior and rule breaking to the modeling effects of portrayals of men's and women's roles. Feminists, desiring to change people's thinking about what are appropriate roles for men and women, have been especially concerned about this effect of television viewing. Studies have indicated that children who watch programs in which women fill roles which have not been customarily filled by women—police detectives and business executives, for instance—are more likely to think these are appropriate roles for women.

As two researchers have put it: "The findings support the assertion that television helps shape children's sex-role perceptions. Children do nominate television characters as people they want to be like when they grow up. There is ample evidence that children can learn through imitation, and it is reasonable to assume that they will imitate particular people whom they say they want to be like. Since children choose [to identify] primarily [with] high-stereotyped characters of their own sex, television must be either directly teaching or reinforcing the stereotypes. . . . Our data on counterstereotypical sex-role portrayals, however, indicate that television might become a potent means of changing stereotypical values in children."[11]

The consistency of research conclusions of this sort has led feminists to bring pressure in the television industry to do exactly what those researchers suggested—to make the medium a potent means of changing children's and adults' thinking about gender roles. The feminists' goal is not only to legitimize the erasure of gender differences. They want to provide new models for girls and women in American society to imitate.

Television, a reflection of the reigning cultural ideals, merely reinforces views that most viewers already have. For example, American television strengthens the perspective that the United

States is the world's leading and most important nation. Television offers models which merely reinforce existing attitudes and behavior; for example, that we should adopt an independent stance against authority. In a period of cultural change, however, television reflects change rather than stability. New ideals and values formed in the culture's opinion-shaping centers are quickly reflected in television programming. The medium then cultivates *changes* in viewers' perspectives and offers them *new* models. This puts television in conflict with established ways of seeing the world and established models of behavior. For example, the ideas and values behind television programs which feature women controlling businesses, out-doing men in physical prowess, and living without dependence on men originate in feminism, a movement which seeks to alter the culture. When television picks up feminist beliefs and values it becomes an agent of change, shaping the views of the many people who have not accepted feminist ways of looking at things.

In cases like this, is television really able to change adults' minds? Can it cause us to see the world anew, reject our old views, and adopt new ways of thinking and living? The answer seems to be: not singlehandedly. Neither experimental evidence or social experience demonstrates that television alone can reverse our thinking and behavior. But, of course, television is almost never in this position. Rather television is always only one of many influences on our thinking and behavior. So the question is whether, in combination with other forces, television plays an effective part in changing our minds. The answer to this question is clearly yes, although it is difficult to determine how much a part it plays.

For example, it is not easy to assess television's role in the growth of conservative politics which began in the 1960s and became ascendent in 1980. By reversing around fifty years of liberal economic policy, the tax cuts and budget revisions of 1981 showed that a genuine national shift to the right was in process, not merely a change of rhetoric or style. Did television's unrelenting scrutiny of the failures of federal government policy disillusion voters with liberal policies? Did the violence of the television world heighten Americans' anxieties about the state of the world, thus strengthening support for a build-up of the military establishment?

However, if television fostered the repudiation of liberal approaches, what are we to make of the long-standing conservative contention that the liberal leanings of the managers of the television networks, the writers and directors of the entertainment industry, and the newsmen have been reflected in their programming? Clearly television played a part in the conservative renaissance, but it was a complex part which could not be reduced simply to a statement about the medium's inherent conservative or liberal tendencies.

It is difficult to sort out television's role in reshaping people's political views because television does not mainly deal in politics. The political implications of much of its entertainment and information are indirect and ambiguous. Game show contestants and detective show policemen do not spend their time unburdening themselves regarding the causes of inflation or the pros and cons of the latest nuclear weapons system. By contrast, the *social* messages of the television world are much more direct, although—as is natural for television—they come across in images and action rather than in argument and discourse. Television is always communicating something about life styles, personal relationships, and values. There are messages about the importance of material possessions, about what behavior is appropriate for men and for women, about what success is, about sexual freedom, about alcohol, drugs, homosexuality, and on and on. If it is difficult to say whether the television world is predominantly liberal or conservative *politically*, it is not so difficult to say whether it is liberal or conservative *socially*. On hardly any of the social topics just named could it be said that television is primarily a conserving influence.

A friend of mine who is a Christian historian is considering writing a book which would have the title *Whatever Happened in 1966?* The book, if he ever writes it, will analyze the revolution in American mores which broke out in the 1960s. A more precise way of putting it would be to say the "marked acceleration" of social change which took place. The rates of divorce, illegitimacy, and premarital sexual activity, which had been slowly rising for decades, took a sudden upturn. People's acceptance of abortion, nontraditional approaches to marriage, homosexual practice, and consciousness-altering drugs increased. Rates of alcoholism, drug addiction, and suicide climbed. A powerful movement to remove all social and political distinctions between men and women appeared. Interest in the occult, supernatural-psychic experiences, and Eastern religions blossomed. In short, broad waves of social change rose up and washed over American culture. The thinking and behavior of a lot of people changed.

Television was hardly in the vanguard. It held back more than it led, largely because of its mass-market audience. Needing to assemble the largest possible audiences for national advertisers, broadcast television has been hesitant to offend, and so has been reluctant to deliberately adopt the role of social change agent. Confronting people's deeply held values is not the best way to sell them deodorants. So television's openness to sexual innuendo in the 1970s, for example, was not the harbinger of a coming sexual revolution but the token of the already widespread abandonment of traditional sexual standards. One observer, citing a 1978 report that in prime time television the incidents of unmarried sexual activity outnumbered married incidents by almost eleven to one, commented, "Network TV can hardly be criticized for reflecting traditional sexual values, although it might be attacked for reflecting contemporary reality."[12]

But if television hesitated to lead the way into social change, it nevertheless played a powerful role in bringing change about. Profound social changes of the kind we are considering have two basic components. The first component consists of changes in the structures of everyday life. The second consists of changes

in beliefs, ideals, values. The rise in sexual promiscuity is an example. Changes in everyday life have played a part; for example, the automobile, which allows unchaperoned dating, and the lengthening of formal education, which keeps people single for longer and creates very loosely structured social environments like college campuses. Changes in values have also played a part, as sex has been removed from the realm of commitment, duty, and service and placed in the realm of self-actualization, personal expression, and recreation.

Television cannot single-handedly produce changes in either structures or ideas. But once these changes are underway, it can accelerate them. It quickly transmits the changes and reinforces them. It acts as a weathervane pointing the direction in which the social winds are blowing. Those who oppose the direction must then struggle against what is popularly perceived as the accepted social trend.

The content of television contributes to changing values and beliefs. Here television has played the part of mediator between the mass society and the cultural centers, where new outlooks and attitudes originate.

Michael Robinson of Catholic University in Washington, D.C., writes:

> Dominant values in much prime-time television, and changes in those dominant values, don't come from the heartland. From civil rights to disco, social movements start in places like New York and L.A., and the media move them out to the boonies. Television gets much of its values and themes from other, classier media (books, and especially magazines), and, to a lesser degree, from an urban-based intelligentsia. Television edits those messages, obviously, before it passes them along as TV chic. But by touching millions, instead of thousands, prime time becomes a highly visible, national, and immediate cause of changing social norms. TV may not be a first cause, but it is a highly apparent one. Prime time helps to make the social values of the coastline elites the social values of the nation.[13]

Robinson's argument is that entertainment television is especially receptive—even if after a cautious lapse of time—to the changing values of particular elite groups. Television powerfully magnifies the trends in these groups and delivers them to virtually every home and member of society. The television reflections thus help to move the entire society in the direction of these trends.

The process has been called homogenization. Every society has subgroups—social classes, people at different levels of education, ethnic groups, religious groups. Subgroups tend to lose their distinctive identities as the media, especially television, reinforce patterns of social change that run contrary to the subgroups' ways of thinking and behaving. Robinson is speaking of this process of homogenization when he refers to movements which begin in centers of the secular culture and which "the media then move out to the boonies." "The boonies" here means all the subgroups in society who have a stake in preserving what the cultural trend-setters want to change. In today's secular society, Christians constitute such a subgroup. Christian patterns of sexual morality and family life, for example, are being rejected throughout the larger society in the schools, the government, the social sciences, entertainment, and popular culture. The distinctive Christian approaches are threatened by the homogenizing effects of television, which undermines all beliefs and values except those of the cultural centers which it reflects.

Robinson offers an explanation of how television actually erodes the views of society's subgroups and replaces them with what he calls TV chic. The way television does it, he contends, is by widening the range of values and behavior which people consider respectable. This is the first step toward their actually embracing the new views and imitating the new models.

For example, Robinson writes that "most critics saw Mary Richards—[Mary Tyler] Moore's *nomme de tube*—as a proto-feminist, at the very least. As a single, sexually interested TV producer Richards was more independent and professional than most mid-thirties American women. . . . Popular sit-com characters, who appear every week, who rarely threaten any-body's ego, who lay their own values down gently and humorously on the coffee table and walk away, have a unique potential for affecting their audiences. . . . The program's values will lead viewers to think that if decent people like Mary Richards act that way, that's probably a legitimate way to behave."[14] By winning acceptance for new patterns as legitimate, television opens the way for people to discuss them and feel more comfortable about adopting them.

A more refined psychological explanation has been offered for the process by which television gains toleration for new social patterns or, more precisely, for the process by which people are detached from their old patterns. This explanation is that when television presents behavior which a person would previously have considered a violation of his beliefs and values, the medium wears away his or her dismay at seeing these values rejected. This, the explanation goes, is a form of desensitization therapy, a behavior modification technique.

Some behavior modification treatment aims at stripping a person of feelings of disturbance and anxiety which he or she has in response to certain stimuli. The goal is to replace the negative feelings with positive ones. For instance, a behavior modification approach to male homosexuality works at desensitizing the man to the female genitals—whittling away at his fears—and providing positive reinforcement for heterosexual relations.

One form of such behavior modification uses images. The client with a phobia or fear is brought into a pleasant and routine atmosphere where he or she feels at ease. Images of the source of distress are presented. When the client begins to experience the usual negative response, the images are withdrawn and the client is allowed to relax again. Food and drink may be provided to help with this. Gradually the client becomes able to view the previously frightening or distressing images for longer periods while remaining relaxed. Eventually an emotionless state develops in response to the images. Then, when the client encounters situations like those pictured in the therapy, he or she is able to deal with them without distress. The images even become associated with pleasant sensations, such as relaxation, eating, and drinking. Not every behavioral and emotional problem is susceptible to this kind of treatment, but it is a potent method for dealing with many difficulties.

Cornell University sociologist Rose Goldsen finds an exact fit between this form of behavior modification and television viewing.[15] Like clinical behavior modification, television is viewed in a relaxed environment—home. Some people even view in bed or in the bath. Television also is viewed with low involvement and alternating interest. Before the viewer's tension or distress becomes too intense, it is interrupted by conversation, the telephone, chores, or, at least, a commercial. Often television viewing is even accompanied by eating and drinking, which helps maintain relaxation and provides positive reinforcement—the association of pleasant feelings with the material which before may have caused distress.

Goldsen notes that behavior modification using images is even more effective if it is accompanied by group discussion. This is consciousness-raising in a technical sense. This aspect too is paralleled in television watching, as viewers casually discuss what they are watching. We may assume that at least a great deal of viewers' comments are positive, since people generally report that they like what they are watching.

How does the process actually work? Goldsen offers the soap operas as an example. Presumably most viewers come to these dramas with deep attachments to family life—feelings of warmth and security regarding the home, an emotional commitment to love being true and marriages working out, an inclination to be protective of children. Consequently we would expect viewers to experience anger, anxiety, or dismay at the sight of homes where family members are not committed to one another, at adultery and divorce, at the presentation of persons manipulating one another, at incest, abortion, child rejection, and the other stuff of soap operas. As Goldsen points out, "Soap-opera people live in a world of fly-apart marriages: throwaway husbands, throwaway wives, and—recently—throwaway lovers. Quite plausibly, the disposable marriage is the source of disposable children. Indeed, the most effective way the soaps do violence to images of family commitment is by a visual code that implicitly denies that children are important in family living. As the episodes spin out their daily show-and-tell, the country is scarcely permitted to see any children at all."[18] In the soaps, pregnancy is usually unwanted. Serial liaisons, uncouplings and recombinations, in wedlock or not, are routine. Speaking ill of other people is the activity which occupies most of people's time. In sum, the soaps' entertainment effect stems almost entirely from their relentless assault on the entire set of emotional attachments which bind family members together.

Of course much great drama has dealt with the transgressing of sacred boundaries and the overcoming of social inhibitions—

and the consequences of such actions. The soaps, however, present the transgressions and escapes from inhibitions as *routine*. The soaps wear away viewers' distress at the violation of deeply held attachments to trust, faithfulness, commitment, honesty, and love in family life. Treating the emotional overtones of this violation as of no consequence, mere gimmicks to keep the plots moving, Goldsen writes, the soaps "reduce all passion to the level of the cheery eulogies to Comet and big-machine Dash that interrupt incessantly. Ignoring the tragic element in the human condition, just passing it by, anesthetizes emotions instead of quickening them: this goes on every day in mass desensitization sessions which soap operas target to the nation's homes."[16]

What is mainly of concern to us here is not soap operas alone, but the dynamics by which they affect us. In fact, the soap operas are only one aspect of television programming which desensitizes us to the violation of Christian beliefs and values.

In many ways television programming works to broaden our thinking, so that we accept viewpoints and behavior which we previously ruled out of bounds. It deadens our reactions to social patterns which we previously found wrong and reacted against. Television cultivates the response, "Well, what I always thought was right turns out not to be right for everyone, at least today. And what I thought was wrong may actually be right for some people. What I used to find shocking maybe isn't so bad. I suppose we have to accept it and learn to live with it." And finally television disinhibits us from actually doing things we would have restrained ourselves from doing. In this way, television has been playing a part in the profound social changes which have been transforming American society since the 1960s.

SEVEN

The Video View of Life

B Y AROUSING US, giving us models, and eroding our resistances, television plants and uproots in the garden of our
minds. The sowing of sexual desires, the obliteration of men's
and women's differences, the desensitizing of emotional
attachments—these dynamics cultivate a certain view of the
world. In these ways television tends to shape our mental
landscape. Despite the variety of television programs, and
despite the variety of sources which produce them, the outlook
on the world which most secular programming fosters has a
unity and consistency. From the soaps to the news, from the
adventures to sports, common themes run throughout secular
television content. Many of these themes run contrary to
Christian thinking.

At this point, where numerous elements of the television
world coalesce into a powerful view of reality, television poses a
great challenge to Christians. Television confronts Christians
with much more than commercials that create material
dissatisfactions or situation comedies that offend with off-color
jokes. Television nourishes a certain non-Christian way of
looking at life.

George Gerbner, of the University of Pennsylvania, writes
that instead of asking what kinds of *specific effects* certain
aspects of television, such as violence, have, we should want to
know what *overall mentality* television cultivates. This, he
writes, is "like asking about the 'effects' of Christianity on one's
view of the world or—as the Chinese had asked—of Con-

fucianism on public morality."[1] In other words, the most important question to ask about television content's effects is, What view of reality does it foster?

In considering television's worldview, the goal is not to inquire into what television may directly lead a person to do, but rather what range of things it may lead him to consider doing, and how it may lead him to evaluate the meaning of what he does. A person's view of the world does not lead directly to action. But depending on his or her worldview, a person will think certain actions are right and others wrong; he will see some issues as important, others as trivial; he will fear some things and hope for others.

For example, a husband and father with a Christian view of the world will regard faithfulness to his wife as a reasonable approach to marriage rather than an unreasonable curb on his personal freedom. He will consider it more important that his children learn about God than about mathematics. He will hope for grace to serve his family more than he looks forward to his next fishing trip. The man's Christian worldview will not cause him to do anything in particular for his wife or children. He will need teaching, models, experience, study, and support to know how exactly to love and serve them and to make the effort to do it. His worldview, however, is the framework for how he relates to them. It sets the direction and boundaries for his actions.

A person's worldview shapes his thoughts and actions because it is his understanding of what is real. A person with an animist worldview will take precautions against malicious spirits when he goes out at night because he accepts the reality of spirits. A Marxist will dedicate his life to the cause of revolution because he sees history in terms of the class struggle and believes the classless society to be an achievable goal. The Christian seeks to obey God's law because he believes God exists and rewards those who trust in him. What a person thinks is real determines ultimately how he will live. All his decisions are made in relation to the way the furniture is arranged in his mental universe. This is not to say that people always do what seems right in terms of their view of reality. But when they do not, their worldview provides the standards by which they measure their failures and assess the consequences.

Does television cultivate a view of reality? The investigations of George Gerbner and his associates shed some interesting light on this question.[2] Their method has been twofold. First, they have studied systematic distortions in the television world. For example, compared to the real world, the television world of entertainment programs has a disproportionate percentage of people involved in law enforcement occupations, fewer children and old people, more professional and upper class people, and a greater likelihood that a person will encounter personal violence. Second, they have surveyed light and heavy television viewers to see whether the heavier viewers are more likely than light viewers to think that the world is as it is presented on television.

This is exactly what they have found. Heavy viewers tend more than light viewers to think the world is the way television shows it to be. For example, heavy viewers are more likely to overestimate the proportion of people who are actually employed in law enforcement work. They are also more likely to think "people cannot be trusted and will take advantage of you if they can." In answer to a wide variety of questions, heavy viewers are more likely to give "television answers." Apparently the more television people watch, the more they think the world is as it seems to be on the screen.

The researchers investigated the possibility that the light and heavy viewers were simply different in age, sex, or education. Perhaps less educated people, who might be more open to television's instruction, happened to watch more television. But television's impact cuts across such differences. For example, when the researchers compared college-educated light viewers with college-educated heavy viewers, it turned out that the heavy viewers were more likely than the light viewers to think the world is as television showed it. Television, in other words, skewed heavy viewers' notions of what the world is like, regardless of their age, sex, or level of education.

*"Friends, we have temporarily lost the video portion of our talk
show but will continue to bring you the inane flummery
of our panelists."*

Gerbner and his fellow researchers have given names to two
effects television has on heavy viewers. The researchers have
called these trends mainstreaming and resonance.

Mainstreaming refers to the phenomenon that television
seems to move viewers with divergent opinions toward a
common or mainstream view. For example, nonwhite people in
the United States are more likely than whites to consider fear of
crime to be a personal problem. Upper class folks are less likely
than the general population to think fear of crime is a personal
problem. So nonwhites and upper class people are, as groups,

above and below the general American level of anxiety about crime. However, nonwhites who are heavy viewers of television tend to be *less* fearful than nonwhites who are light viewers. And upper income folks who are heavy television watchers are *more* fearful of crime than upper income folks who do not watch a lot of television. Thus heavy viewing seems to move nonwhites and upper class people toward a common, mainstream level of anxiety about crime.

Resonance, as the researchers use the term, means that television can magnify attitudes viewers already have. For example, people who live in high-crime areas naturally tend to be more fearful of crime than folks who live in safer areas. But heavy viewers who live in high crime areas are *especially* fearful—more fearful than light viewers in those areas. The television worldview resonates powerfully in viewers' thinking when it portrays situations which are already on their minds.

Other studies have shown that television has an effect on people's knowledge of what is involved in carrying out various occupations and influences people's ideas of how prestigious certain occupations are. This, of course, is an important part of a person's grasp of the social order he or she lives in. In one investigation, children and parents were more likely to give similar prestige rankings to occupations they saw on television than occupations they had contact with in real life. Television evidently was shaping their views of what kinds of work are more and less important. The researchers referred to this phenomenon as a "homogenization effect." They saw television providing commonly accepted but superficial and misleading information about the labor force which could lead to difficult personal and social problems as children grew up and entered the adult world of work.[3]

Some research has focused on television's power to cultivate perspectives in the political realm. One group of researchers has written: "In politics, television appears to affect knowledge and information and to define the context in which voting decisions are made. Along with the other mass media, it helps to establish the agenda of personalities and issues to which the public responds. Television has an important role because it is the ultimate mass medium focusing the nation's attention on the same topics, persons, and messages."[5]

An example of this kind of agenda setting is the public's concern about law-and-order issues. For instance, a Cambridge Survey Research study in the early 1970s found that even residents of small rural towns in Wisconsin, New Hampshire, Oregon, and Nebraska, where there was virtually no local violent crime, rated crime in the streets as "one of the major issues in our community."[5] In cases such as this, television is not necessarily influencing voters to pull a particular lever on election day but is shaping the concerns which politicians will emphasize and voters will attend to.

One intriguing study tried to measure the effects of television and films on young people's perceptions of sexual experience. The researchers sought to determine whether there was a connection between viewers' perception of media characters' sexual exploits as real and viewers' feelings of satisfaction with their own sexual experience. The study consisted of a survey of undergraduates at a state university in 1976. The students were asked if they thought that media portrayals of sexual behavior were realistic, whether they thought that media characters enjoyed their sexual experience more than they did themselves, and other questions.

Students who had not yet engaged in sexual intercourse were more likely to be dissatisfied with their sexual state if they thought that movie portrayals of sexual activity were realistic. The results regarding television were inconclusive. In 1976 television was not showing much explicit sexual activity. So students' evaluations of the realism of sexually explicit material on television were based on relatively little material.

The researchers concluded: "Media presentations of sexual behavior were an important factor in an individual's satisfaction as a virgin. Those who saw movie portrayals of sex as being real and those who saw media characters as experiencing greater sexual satisfaction reported less satisfaction in their own state of virginity. As predicted, the media may indeed serve as a contributing factor to an individual's picture of his or her sexual self. The virgin is forced to deal with peer pressure regarding his or her virginity, but apparently must also face and react to mass media pressures as well."[6] In the years since this study, television has become somewhat more explicit regarding sexual activity, especially on cable. It is therefore reasonable to think that television is increasingly playing the same role as movies in cultivating young single people's dissatisfaction with lack of sexual experience.

There are, then, strong indications that television contributes to the shaping of our views of reality—how affluent people are, how dangerous the world is, how satisfying sexual experience is, and so on. These perspectives, in turn, give rise to particular opinions and attitudes. For example, crime becomes a leading political issue throughout the nation; lack of sexual experience becomes a matter of heightened dissatisfaction.

As one among many factors, it is impossible to measure the precise contribution that television makes to the formation of our views of the world. It is clear, however, that television has some effect. As Gerbner and his associates write, "The observable independent contributions of television can only be relatively small. But just as an average temperature shift of a few degrees can lead to ice age or the outcome of elections can be determined by slight margins, so too can a relatively small but pervasive influence make a crucial difference. The 'size' of an 'effect' is far less critical than the direction of its steady contribution."[7]

Like a prevailing wind pattern which interacts with temperature, land formations, and water to form a region's climate, television makes a low-intensity, diffuse, constant contribution to people's thinking about how the world is. Universally available, attended to for so many hours by virtually everyone, accessible to young children and other people who do not read or do not want to read, television has a mind-shaping influence on us that is unique among the institutions in our society.

Our notions of how dangerous the world is, how prestigious

various occupations are, or how satisfying sexual activity is form important parts of our view of reality. However, these are not necessarily the most important points at which television shapes our thinking. Television also communicates numerous, less obvious, and even more value laden messages about the world. The effects of these messages on our thinking are hard to determine. However, the indications that television affects people's thinking in the more obvious areas supports the supposition that television's less obvious messages are also having an impact on us.

Television presents us not with reality itself but with significant pictures of reality. We have seen how television affects us simply because it is realistic—we see real human beings in realistic or actual settings. However, television is also more than realistic. Its selections of images of reality have levels of meaning that extend beneath the surface.

Violence provides an example. On the first level of meaning, televised violence is simply violence. We understand it for what it is. Watching a lot of it shapes our thinking. The more we watch, the more we tend to think that the world is violent, and that we should be suspicious of other people we encounter.

But beneath this surface level of meaning, television violence signifies other things. Violence is always part of a story in which good and evil are in conflict. Knowing this, we respond to televised violence differently from actual violence. Real violence usually activates feelings of shock, fear, or horror. By contrast television violence mainly triggers two emotions—anger at the violence of the bad guys and satisfaction at the violence of the good guys. We are responding not to the violence itself but to the playing out of a conflict of good and evil.

Television often associates certain qualities with the successful use of violence. In a study conducted several years ago, George Gerbner noted that the ratio of killers to corpses varied from one group to another in the television world. Among white Americans, there were four killers for every one killed. Among white foreigners there were three killers for every two killed. Among nonwhite Americans, there was one killer for every one killed. In other words, white Americans were seen to be efficient and successful in the use of violence and unlikely to be victims. Nonwhite Americans, by comparison, were seen as more bungling in the use of violence and more likely to be preyed upon. Gerbner noted that in addition to efficiency, a cool unemotionalism, manliness, and youthfulness were associated with the successful use of violence.[8]

This kind of analysis shows that violence on television communicates more than the perception that the world is a violent place. It also teaches about qualities which are most valued in the culture—Americanness, whiteness, manliness, coolness, efficiency, and youthfulness. The violence on television often represents the conflict between these qualities and qualities which the culture regards as less important or less central—being foreign, nonwhite, womanly, emotional, inefficient, or old. Thus while television programs portray violence in ways that are considered realistic, they also mirror the prevailing values in American society. When we experience satisfaction at the triumph of the good guys using violence on television, we are applauding the success of good over evil *as defined in the television world.* We are applauding the assertion of American values over values which conflict with them.

The patterns of association with violence are not the only clue to the multilayered meanings of much television violence. Another clue is the stylized presentations of violence. While violence in real life often happens between people who know one another well, such as angry family members, television violence normally happens between strangers. While real-life violence often results in excruciating pain with long-lasting effects, television violence is comparatively bloodless, painless, and fast. It often kills, but it rarely results in prolonged agony. These stylizations of violence suggest that violence itself is not the only matter of concern, but that violence points to things beyond itself. The stylizations of violence on television are similar to the masks which ancient Greek actors wore. The masks made it plain that the characters represented something more important than themselves. The play pointed to larger unseen realities.

The purpose of examining violence is not to condemn television programmers for offering entertainment and news which show violence. Throughout history, violent popular stories have carried messages about the values that particular societies most respected. What is important to note at this point is simply that even the most realistic-seeming television programming carries unsuspected messages. There are depths below the screen's glistening surface.

If television communicates messages on more than one level at once, what are the messages that it is conveying? While television seems to present a wide variety of programs—an assortment that is growing wider with the addition of cable channels—much of television is marked by a repetitiveness and sameness. This is simply because television is a popular medium. Popular cultural forms, such as popular music, are always characterized by a limited range of characters, images, and stories. Television, for all its showy variety and newness, constantly returns to the same themes.[9]

Indeed, television, which seems at first to be so realistic, turns out on closer examination to be composed of numerous standard parts which are fitted together in many slightly different but basically similar combinations. Television speaks with a limited vocabulary. It employs stock characters: the faithful man Friday, the tough, wise-cracking physician, the attractibe young woman with more bosom than brains, the shifty-eyed, small-town big-wig, the sexually interested, ever-frustrated young man, the snobbish intellectual, the effeminate clergyman, the dim-witted husband and his sharp-witted wife. Such characters have become familiar through repetition. The list could be extended to include stereotyped presentations of politicians on the news, participants on game shows, characters in the soaps, experts on the talk shows.

These stock characters have typical stories. The man Friday plays a crucial but undramatic part in the adventure. The tough physician is inevitably involved in a bittersweet romance. The small-town politico is discovered to be an embezzler. With this limited vocabulary of characters and stories, television speaks a limited number of underlying messages to almost all the homes in the land. Here are a few.

1. Life is a search for lasting relationships.

Example: A made-for-television movie offers the story of a divorced woman, the divorced man who lives with her, her teenage daughter, and the daughter's boyfriend. The woman's act of unfaithfulness to the man she is living with (can this be called adultery?) almost wrecks their relationship. The daughter's aggressiveness with her boyfriend almost scares him away. Finally mom confesses her underlying insecurities to her housemate, and the daughter and boyfriend reach an understanding about the timing of their relationship.

Example: In another television movie, the demolition of a sorority house uncovers the skeleton of an aborted child. The six likely suspects live in town. The twenty-five years since their college graduation have been crowded with disappointments and betrayals, mostly from men. The threat of a court investigation of the skeleton now draws them together. At last one of them admits she had the abortion and dropped the baby down the air shaft. All the women pledge to testify that they did it. In the final scene the women walk up the courthouse steps arm in arm.

Example: In a third movie, various women who are unknown to each other share a common affliction—husbands who beat them. The women end up together at a sanctuary for battered wives. In sensitivity sessions they learn to speak honestly about their lives and how they feel about them.

Comment: The drama of these movies consists in the trials encountered by people as they attempt to find deep, lasting bonds, whether with members of the opposite or the same sex, whether sexually active or not. The stories assume that lasting human relationships are very difficult to achieve. At first the characters are unsuccessful in seeking secure relationships, because they are not honest about their feelings. Then they honestly share about their feelings, and sexual relationships are restored and sisterhood is established. Thus a second message is communicated which is a corollary of the first: When personal relationships deteriorate it is largely because people are not being honest about their feelings.

2. New forms of behavior are to be welcomed.

Example: A local news program reports on the proliferation of video games establishments in the area. It contrasts the efforts of a mother and teenage daughter to limit the growth of the industry in their town with the enthusiasm of patrons and proprietors of video games places. The mother and daughter are shown to fill perfectly the role of uptight conservators of the past. The video games fans appear as lovers of harmless fun.

Example: A news special looks at surrogate mothers—women who, for a fee, consent to be artificially inseminated by men whose wives cannot conceive, and to bear children for the childless couple. A couple are shown in their living room with a child they obtained this way. The child plays with toys. In another scene, a psychiatrist states that the surrogate parents she knows would be indistinguishable from anyone else at a cocktail party.

Example: A comedy presents a crusty father of two teenage daughters who want more freedom to go off and experience the world. A cousin comes to visit; she is a walking embodiment of the counterculture the girls long to explore. The cousin is obnoxious, angers her uncle, and he orders her to leave. Finally, however, he realizes he is mistaken: she is simply the product of insufficient mothering. Her rude behavior is quite excusable. He is the one who has been unreasonable.

Comment: Television propagandizes for the new. In the first case, it seems, the newsmen have honestly tried to show both sides of the videogame story, but the cultural bias against limitations on new kinds of behavior controls the presentation. The camera dwells lovingly on its electronic sibling—the video game equipment. The newsmen do not use their medium to create a visually effective case against the proliferation of establishments where children can spend ever more time out of the sight of their parents.

The other two examples are less innocent examples of the cultural bias in favor of new modes of behavior. The report on surrogate mothering does not challenge the practice on moral grounds. In fact, the program gives the new practice a boost by making it seem familiar: surrogate mothering may seem unusual, but here are the ordinary men, women, and children involved in it.

The third example presents a clear instance of light-weight entertainment making a social statement. As the representative of older ways, the father is shown to be hard-hearted. In the person of the niece, the new ways are shown to be merely the excusable outworkings of ordinary family difficulties—hardly anything to draw the line against.

3. Sex underlies everything.

Example: Deodorants and mouthwash, soft drinks and beer, automobiles, clothing, airline tickets, and whole wheat bread are promoted with images of partially clothed men and women in romantic situations.

Example: A comedy plays on twin misunderstandings. A young woman mistakenly believes a young man is giving a married woman instructions in sexual technique, while he is really giving her cooking lessons. Meanwhile the young man believes the young woman is being set up by a doctor as a mistress, while the doctor is really arranging an apartment for his niece.

Example: A daily game show probes the details of newlyweds' thoughts and feelings about each other, offering viewers glimpses of the couples' sexual behavior.

Comment: The "sexual assumption"—the belief that everything in life leads ultimately to sex—is one of the most pervasive of television's messages. It is so truly pervasive that examples are almost unnecessary. Certainly the message that resonates in all the examples here is that everyone is always thinking about sex. Goods and services are desirable because they provide ways to shed sexual anxieties and achieve sexual satisfaction. People are always thinking of each other in terms of sexual activity. The most interesting aspects of people's lives are their sexual experiences.

4. *The best people are young, efficient, affluent, and urban.*

Example: A married detective couple, rich city dwellers, head for their cabin in the mountains only to become enmeshed in a case of murder in the nearby small town. Some of the local people are victims of murder and frame-up. Others among the locals, including the sheriff, are the villains. The glamorous couple rescue the helpless local folks and bring the sheriff and his accomplice to justice.

Example: A comedy features two single women who have moved to California to find a new life but are both locked into dull jobs, a less-than-classy social circle, and a tacky apartment. Faced with an invitation to a high school class reunion, one of the women reviews her failure to achieve wealth and status. The other woman comforts her with the assurance that she is doing her best and should be proud of herself.

Comment: Ben Stein, in *The View from Sunset Boulevard,* explores the outlook of the less than 500 people, residents of the

Los Angeles area, who are the writers and directors of most of the original entertainment material seen on network television. He finds that among the common traits in their thinking are a distrust of big business and small towns, and an admiration for people who are like themselves—talented, successful, urban, and affluent.[10]

The first example here offers a transparent instance of how violence in television programming carries messages. The murder mystery shows how smart and efficient those glamorous city people can be.

The second example is more subtle. On the face of it, the message is that the two lower-middle-class working women are to mystery shows how smart and efficient those glamorous be commended for their struggle to make it. The message is ambiguous, however. Should the viewer see them as successful? They have moved to California just like many other folks in the last few decades, undoubtedly including many of the people who have written, directed, and produced the program. But while these other folks have made it, the two women have not. While it is possible to see the program as an affirmation of the women's efforts, it is also possible to see it as a joke at their expense: How amusing! Two patently unsuccessful people feeling proud of themselves. However one interprets the message, it is clear that the program's definition of success is the glamorous good life in California.

5. *The world is moved by the struggles of strong individuals.*

Example: For several weeks, evening newscasts portray a complicated policy vote before the Congress as a personal challenge to the President. His prestige is on the line. "He refuses to predict that he will win." Is he strong enough to persuade the congressmen to go along with him? Which congressmen will give in to presidential pressures? How will they explain that they have had their arms twisted?

Example: An evening news report includes items about the arrest of terrorists in New York City, former federal employees involved in undercover operations with a foreign government, and school millage battles. All the reports focus on a few individual people involved, such as a woman who was arrested in New York and the president of a board of education.

Comment: While the element of personal challenge to the President is actually present in the matter before Congress, that is not in fact the main issue. However, the cultural tendency to reduce social conflicts to combat between individual accords perfectly with television's need to present visually dramatic material which shows the texture of individuals' personal style and their emotional reactions.

All the examples communicate the message that individuals— not institutions, social classes, or interest groups—are in control of society. The reports on the terrorists and the collaborators also carry a corollary message: Social problems are due to a few criminal individuals.

6. *People are just folks.*

Example: Some of the material already described carries this message. The crotchety father and his counterculture niece are shown not to be exponents of contradictory approaches to life. They are really just a hard-head with a well-hidden soft heart and a nice girl with some odd tastes. The people involved in surrogate mothering are also just ordinary people.

Example: A comedy about a medical station in the Korean war involves a straight colonel, a cynical, egotistical doctor ("I can show you a room full of women as lack-of-character witnesses"), a snobbish doctor, and an aging vaudeville queen. The colonel turns out to be a chivalrous romantic. The cynical doctor scrupulously avoids taking advantage of a young female patient. The snobbish doctor enjoys a little popular dancing. The

vaudeville queen is, after all, like the older woman next door—
good-hearted and lonely.

Comment: Under the surface, everyone is a regular guy or gal.
People have their hang-ups and eccentricities, but they are all
basically good. They are, in fact, all really middle-class
Americans. American cultural values are universal. Harmony in
the world is therefore possible.

7. The government is out of touch with the people and impotent, but many of the individuals in the government are sharp, well-trained, and capable.

Example: One evening a Canadian newscast features stories
about (1) the closing of some passenger rail lines, with pictures
of angry M.P.'s and local politicians; (2) a national-provincial
oil and gas agreement, with pictures of local businessmen who
are being driven into bankruptcy by it; (3) a marooned freighter
that some government agencies are impounding while other
agencies are trying to get rid of, with pictures of local residents
who express dismay with the eyesore; (4) a general who is
worried that citizens do not understand national defense policy;
(5) an I.R.A. bombing in London, England, with pictures of the
cool-headed officer in charge of the investigation; and (6)
Haitian refugees drowned on the Florida coast, with pictures of
the state's governor saying that he hopes the disaster will finally
spur the government to take necessary actions to avert such
tragedies.

Comment: All these reports fit into a remarkably consistent
pattern. In every case the government is shown to be un-
responsive to the needs of ordinary people or out of touch with
them. This does not seem to be the fault of bad intentions.
Rather, it is implied, the government is inherently unable to
deal effectively with problems. Once again, however, the role of

the strong individual is stressed—especially individuals who are affluent, urban, and efficient.

The messages we have considered are some of the more prominent but hardly the only messages that secular television programming communicates. For the most part, their presence on television is not the result of deliberate propagandizing, although there is certainly some of that. Rather television picks up the cultural values and perspectives of the leading groups in society—particularly those of the more affluent, educated, urban, and secularist elements—and mirrors them through its repertoire of stock characters and stories, fictional and non-fictional. The result is a system of messages that reflects the predominant secular culture.

The composite view of the world that secular television cultivates is, in one sense, very inaccurate. Television does not show the world as it is in such matters as the levels of violence and affluence in American society. In another sense, however, television mirrors society quite well. Beneath its surface, television communicates a system of messages which show contemporary society's anxieties about personal relationships (message 1), its relativistic approach to behavior (message 2), its preoccupation with sex (message 3), its admiration for youth and efficiency (message 4), its individualism (messages 5 and 7), its conviction that people are basically okay (message 6), and so on. In its representation of popular American values and concerns, television is remarkably accurate. Indeed, for a picture of what is going on in Americans' heads and personal lives, there is hardly a better place to go than television.

This is where television's worldview affects our thinking most strongly. The greatest problem is not television material that is consciously designed to change our thinking. The greatest problems lie in the material that simply reflects the reigning cultural perspectives. The reason is that the culture is not Christian.

EIGHT

Television and the Christian Mind

THE ASSUMPTIONS of contemporary society contrast sharply with Christian perspectives. For instance, while open to change and material progress, the Christian is not infinitely receptive to all new forms of human behavior. He knows that some ways of acting are in accord with God's will for men and women while other ways are not. (In fact, the Christian recognizes that some of what parades as new behavior is really quite old behavior dressed up in new rationales.)

Neither ought the Christian to identity with many of the *concerns and anxieties* of contemporary society. The tortuous search for secure personal relationships is unfortunately a fact of life for very many people today. But it ought not to be a characteristic of Christians' lives, because Christians ought to find stability, faithfulness, and mutual service in the home and the church community. The fact that many Christians do not experience such security and instead experience the troubled odyssey toward lasting relationships points to the weakness of lived Christianity today. Similarly, the cultural preoccupation with and anxiety about sex ought to be foreign to the Christian, who has been given clear rules for the proper purpose and place of sex and has inherited a wealth of practical wisdom about handling sex as an important but subordinate part of life. Again, the fact that many Christians do share the culture's virtual obsession with sex is a sign of the weakness of lived Christianity in America today. Immersion in television's expressions of these concerns and anxieties, of course, only enlarges them.

The other side of the coin is equally a problem. Television not only communicates some messages that, while accurately reflecting the culture, are untrue. It also excludes from view a great deal that is true and important. Television clashes with the Christian mind not only in what it says but also in what it does not say.

Simply put, the television worldview—what we might call the television mind—ignores God. It ignores the dynamics of life which are rooted in God or which God has chosen to reveal. The desires and feelings it arouses are often directed toward ends which are different from the ones he has planned. The models it presents are of men and women who live without him. The resistances and inhibitions it erodes are often the ones which men and women who want to obey him ought to have. The messages it communicates stem from a view of the world that assumes God is nonexistent, remote, or unimportant. In short, television is an agnostic. The massive realities of the Christian revelation, which in the scriptural view tower over the landscape like gigantic monuments, are all but invisible to television's nearsighted eye.

We know that the entire universe owes its existence to God. This is of practical importance. Knowing that the universe has been created does more than satisfy our curiosity: it determines the direction of our lives. Since God has created all things, it is our duty to seek his purposes for what he has made and obey his laws.

In the television view, however, it is of no importance whether God made all things or not. Documentaries probe political and economic issues without posing questions such as, What are God's purposes in this area of life, and how can men and women best serve them? In television entertainment's world of police stations and fancy apartments, no one speaks of creation or, apparently, thinks of it. Just as the television world is peopled by higher proportions of law enforcement workers, professionals, and affluent folks than the real world, it is also inhabited by a race of people who for the most part do not care whether they are living in a purposive creation or a cosmic accident.

Because he believes in God the creator, the Christian values certain activities—such as striving to understand and obey God's will. This means that the reading of scripture and the study of Christian teaching are high on the Christian's list of important activities. The Christian also esteems the quality of submissiveness to God's authority—a willingness to learn his ways and keep them. The Christian values traits such as faithfulness and obedience.

The television view is blind to the search for the creator's purposes. Creative man, not creator God, fills the screen. When was the last time a late-night talk show featured a guest whose prominence lay in his uncompromising obedience to God? Guests are not chosen for their exemplary submission to God's will or their keen understanding of his intentions for some department of life. They are chosen for *their* creativity, their own original achievements, their striking expressions of individuality. Self-sufficient men and women are at the center of television's attention. Television trains the viewer to seek wisdom about life only in experts or within himself; seeking wisdom from above, as St. James writes of it, plays no part in the process of living.

Daily Christian life flows from an awareness of being a creature, made with a purpose, cared for by God. This consciousness ought to suffuse the Christian's outlook as blood courses through his veins. The praise and thankfulness which follow this knowledge are marks of the Christian way. But for many of us, this awareness of God's goodness is submerged by the stream of images from the television which, while rising occasionally to heights of technical artistry in showing this beautiful world of movement and color, nowhere relates its fragmented images to the Artist who lies behind them.

Anyone who dips even here and there into scripture cannot help but be struck by the way the people of the Bible lived with a

Cary Grossman

"That's a window, honey. There are no commercials."

personal knowledge that God acts, God works out his plans, God delivers and executes judgment. By contrast, many Christians today sense only weakly the way that God intervenes in the world and each individual's life. Most Christians find it difficult to develop a daily awareness of God as sovereign Lord who holds the initiative in his dealings with us. This difficulty is worsened as we immerse ourselves in the television view of the world, which completely excludes an awareness of God's ability to work his will in every circumstance of life.

On television, God never does anything. No made-for-television movie leaves the viewer marveling at how God worked out everything for the good of the characters who trusted him. No television hero, in a moment of humility, admits his inability to right an injustice and calls on God to act.

No news commentator reflects on the rise and fall of nations in light of the biblical prophets who spoke about the kinds of behavior which God rewards and punishes.

Contemporary life is marked by a sense of distance from God. This is true not only of nonbelievers but of many Christians. Most of us have a clearer idea of what we are doing for God than what he himself is doing. How striking it is to hear someone talk about "what God is doing in the world today," rather than merely what God wants us to be doing. Yet a Christian mind should have a lively sense of God's initiative. The Christian life should be oriented by an ability to perceive what God is doing and to invest ourselves in it. We should follow the example of Christ, who said, "The Son can do only what he sees the Father doing."

Immersion in the television view of the world only makes worse our difficulties developing this outlook. Our failure to see God's hand in the world stems from a spiritual blindness within us. But when we give over our eyes and mind to the television world, we are confirmed in our blindness. Television *trains* us not to see God's hand.

In a war novel, a pilot decides to fly on and complete his mission despite a mechanical failure that makes it certain that afterwards he will not be able to return safely to base. In a movie, a schoolteacher makes an unpopular recommendation to have one of her students expelled. In a television program, a prosecutor oversteps the bounds of professional conduct to secure evidence against an underworld figure. Whether on television or in any other form, much of the entertainment of stories hinges on moral choices such as these. The drama turns on the characters' selection of good or evil, courage or cowardice. By offering us examples of moral choices and their consequences, entertainment can sharpen our moral sensibilities. It can exercise our faculty of distinguishing right from wrong.

The disappointment of television, however, is that it usually dulls rather than sharpens viewers' sense of right and wrong. It confuses more than it clarifies. In one story, a boy feigns blindness to escape a brutal father and win adoption in a better home—a powerful case for lying, made at an emotional level which resists rational refutation. In another story, a married soldier far from home enters an adulterous liaison with a woman of great sensitivity—again, a powerful emotional case for wrongdoing. Such programming makes it harder rather than easier to see what is right about righteousness and wrong about wrongdoing.

This moral confusion weakens the conviction that *any* behavior can be seriously and profoundly wrong. The television world is familiar with failures that are to be regretted, such as soap opera characters making messes of their marriages. And it shows many crimes that deserve to be punished. But what television generally lacks is a sense of *sin*. The enormity of sin escapes the camera's notice.

The Christian has more than a moral code. He or she recognizes the gravity of wrongdoing—its ungratefulness, its wickedness, its eternal folly. The Christian ought to be angered at serious sin. As one writer, Stephen Clark, has noted, Christians are too often angry about that which offends *them* and complacent about that which offends *God*. We are angered more at being cut off on the expressway than by abuse directed at God's law. This shows a failure to develop a fully Christian mentality which sees serious wrongdoing as the personal affront to God which, in fact, it is.

This does not mean thinking or acting judgmentally of others. The Lord himself, in his life on earth, perfectly exemplified anger at sin and mercy to sinners. Indeed the Lord's example teaches that true mercy is possible only when we are aware of sin's gravity. Better to lose eye or hand, our Lord says; better to have a millstone tied around one's neck . . . better never to have been born. . . . Here indeed is a somber assessment of human wrongdoing—more to be dreaded than maiming or drowning. It teaches a fear of sin. Mercy is not toleration of serious sin. When the Christian sees serious wrongdoing, his deepest response is anger combined with a fear for the one committing it and a prayer for God's mercy.

Few of us have been trained in such responses to serious sin. No doubt our minds have been affected by spending many hours on the moral tableland of the television world, where sin has been flattened into insignificance, rather than in the scriptural world, where the collision of righteousness and evil has carved a landscape of soaring peaks and dizzying chasms.

In many cases our thinking also lacks a grasp of the dynamics of good and evil. We might have the right beliefs—that sin is the root problem of the world, that human society apart from God is locked into a system of evil which scripture calls "the world," that human society has fallen under the power of "the prince of this world." But to a larger extent we have not integrated this knowledge in our minds. Our thinking has not been refashioned so that we are able to see our families, careers, and workplaces in these terms.

Here too, television has played its part in our failure to develop a Christian mind. As we have seen, one of secular programming's frequent messages is that "people are just folks." Another message is that people who are young, efficient, and affluent can succeed. The depths of sin in our hearts and the strength of the dominion of evil in the world are thoughts too high or deep to fit in the narrow confines of the secular television world. As television sees it, the world has its problems, but they are not beyond the power of well-intentioned, highly trained individuals to deal with.

If television cannot cope with sin, neither can it face up to redemption. It tells us that life can be improved but not transformed. The absence in television of the biblical critique of mankind's desperate state goes hand in hand with a pre-disposition to deny the possibility of a radical solution. Both the scriptural revelation of sin and the news of its conquest are alien to the television mind.

One of television's underlying messages is "the world is the world is the world." This is all there is, and this is all there is going to be. On the one hand, it's not so bad, television says: situation comedies show us that deep down, everyone is well-intentioned; documentaries show us good, competent people hard at work to bring progress. But don't hope for anything radically better: the soaps display people's endless, tedious unfaithfulnesses; the news reveals society's central institution— the government—as incapable of controlling the course of events.

The television view of the world is similar to some schools of modern psychology. These theories view man without taking into account either original sin or re-creation in Christ. They examine what can go wrong in the psyche of fallen man; and they propose what can be done short of starting all over. Similarly television presents human society without illuminating either its bondage to evil or redemption in Christ. Psychological journals do not offer case studies of how men and women have died in Christ and been raised to new life with God. Television does not dramatize their stories.

The gospel is a shattering announcement: The ordinary ways of the world have been brought under God's judgment; the axe is laid to the root of the tree. God's authority has been reasserted; Jesus is seated at the right hand of God. Men and women are summoned to a life of holiness. The gospel promises not mere improvement but personal transformation. It offers death to this life and resurrection to a new one. The good news is that God is not concerned merely with correcting external behavior but with our total re-creation. St. Paul writes, "It does not matter if a person is circumcised or not. What matters is for him to become an altogether new creature."

This radical message ought to transform our entire outlook on the world. St. Paul writes, "From now on we regard no one from a human point of view. Even though we once regarded Christ from a human point of view, we regard him thus no longer. Therefore, if any one is in Christ, he is a new creation; the old has passed away, behold, the new has come." In light of the new creation which is present in Christ, St. Paul declares that his view of everyone has been revolutionized. From now on, he sees that the world contains two kinds of men and women—those who are a new creation in Christ, and those who are yet invited to become part of that new creation.

An awareness of God's new creation already present among us brings with it a desire to know its full extent: "[May] you have a spirit of wisdom and of revelation in the knowledge of him, having the eyes of your hearts enlightened, that you may know what is the hope to which he called you, what are the riches of his glorious inheritance in the saints, and what is the immeasurable greatness of his power in us who believe." The Christian is meant to live with a consciousness of the might and power of Christ at work among his redeemed people.

Television offers no aid toward developing this mentality. The taking on of a new nature is a process of which television knows nothing. It is ignorant of both the need and the possibility.

Christian critiques of television have appeared since the industry's early years. Christians' criticism of the medium has often shed light on the structures of their own thought. When we confront the central medium of the culture, we expose our own cultural assumptions.

We find examples of this dynamic is some of the manuals published in recent years which attempt to help Christians develop an awareness of the television's shortcomings. Some of these manuals are designed for group study and discussion, for example, *Growing with Television,* which presents itself as "A Study of Biblical Values and the Television Experience." The study series scores television for its images of the American Dream ("There is a deemphasis on wide-ranging problems like those of the urban poor, and there is the implication that technology can solve all problems"). The manual asserts that television confuses fantasy and reality ("Discipleship requires searching for reality"). The manual criticizes the medium for its consumerism, oversimplifications, and other familiar issues.[1]

For the most part, *Growing with Television* touches on real problems. It criticizes some secular values and affirms some Christian ones (it also baptizes some secular values). What is notable, however, is the series' limited vision. "In the Christian faith," the manual explains, "the good life does not consist of getting and having, but of serving and taking care of." "Jesus plainly taught that discipleship requires giving up, not laying up, wealth." These, of course, are truisms of the Christian life. But one looks in vain for the larger perspective in which the Lord taught them. "Do not lay up treasure on earth—lay it up in heaven," he said. "Lay down your life for my sake—so you will keep it for everlasting life." The Lord always situated the demands of discipleship in the context of the kingdom of God, as it was already present in him, but also as it was to come eternally. This perspective of looking beyond the present life to the kingdom to come is strangely absent in *Growing with Television.* The book offers a critique of television's view of happiness—without countering it with Christian hope. The book accuses television of confusing fantasy with reality—without directing the participant's gaze beyond this world to the reality which will endure. The book speaks from a generally Christian position regarding values but is an unfortunate example of Christian thinking infected by secularism. Its perspective, however good, is limited to this world.

In our examination of television programming we have often characterized it as "secular." It is now worth giving some thought to the meaning of the word. "Secular" comes from a Latin word meaning "age." In English, "secular" refers to this present age, as opposed to the world to come. Secularism is a view of life which sees only this visible, natural world and considers any other order of reality unimportant or nonexistent.

We have been applying the term secular to the world of television by way of a kind of shorthand. The television view of reality is at odds with Christianity in many ways, as we have seen. But to say it is "secular" is to touch at once on all the ways that the medium implicitly repudiates the realities of revelation—God as purposeful creator and intervener, the nature of mankind's predicament, and the re-creation in Christ. All these realities presuppose an order of existence above the natural world, an age beyond this "saeculum."

Thus the failure of *Growing with Television* to confront the medium's pervasive secularism is no minor oversight. The manual, which, of course, is only an example of much Christian criticism of television, attempts to retain Christian values while uprooting them from their place in God's eternal kingdom. These Christian critics have implicitly adopted a secularist view of life—that man's chief concern is to improve life in this world. Their argument with television is over the fact that it presents a consumerist, exploitative, uncharitable view of life in this world. Over the issue of man's ultimate destiny—whether it is in this age or the age to come—they have laid down their weapons and are silent.

This capitulation of well-meaning Christians to an essentially secular outlook demonstrates, perhaps more clearly than anything else, the power with which contemporary society promotes its perceptions of reality. A secular current flows powerfully through all the major institutions of our society—government, school, business, the media. Christians do not easily maintain a biblical worldview against this current. In American society today it is not easy to speak publicly, or even think, about events in light of eternity. Whereas in the past Christianity faced the difficulties of extricating itself from paganism and superstition, today it faces the challenge of maintaining a supernatural, eternal perspective on human life.

Once again, the problem for many of us is that our beliefs have not changed our thinking. We believe in eternity, but we do not see our lives and society from an eternal perspective. "How will this matter look in the long run, at the judgment? How then will I wish I had acted now?" "How does Christian hope change the way I must view this suffering?" Our minds too rarely run down such channels.

By its nature, *secular* television blocks the development of this fully Christian mentality. Television presents images of this world in a way that says, This is all there is. The mind remains trapped in the ideals, desires, and anxieties of this life. These are what Malcolm Muggeridge calls "diversions" from the path of faith in God. Muggeridge puts it forcefully: "I think that diversions are more difficult to deal with than ever before because the fantasies of life have been given such extraordinary outward and visible shape, even to the point where you see them on the TV screen for three or four hours a day, these fantasies of power, of leisure, of carnality. Western men and women live in that world of images almost as long as any other, and it is a fearful thing. That is why you find among the young this extraordinary despair, because they feel there is no escape for them—no escape into reality."[2]

Muggeridge is a severe critic of television. While many Christians in recent years have undergone a secularizing of their thinking, he is an example of the traffic in the other direction—a secular man who in later life discovered the truth of Christianity and has undergone a desecularization of his thinking. Perhaps as a result of his late adult conversion, Muggeridge, more than many life-long Christians, has an acute awareness of the clash between secular television and the Christian revelation. The harshest charge he has leveled against the medium is that it is an offense against the first commandment. Television, he writes, is the making and worship of graven images.[3]

In practice Muggeridge qualifies this condemnation. He freely admits that television was an instrument of his own conversion as he helped produce programs on the Holy Land and Mother Teresa of Calcutta. He has also supported the efforts of a Roman Catholic priest in the United States to raise money for some Christian programs—a sign that Muggeridge does not regard television as totally unredeemable. But even with these modifications, Muggeridge's charge is striking. The worship of graven images—the accusation rouses us from our comfortable, mildly entertained position before the screen with the assertion that we are giving our allegiance to a false god.

In fact, as dramatic as Muggeridge's expression may be, it is no more than a summary of the survey we have made of the collision between the Christian mind and the television mind. The hours we spend absorbing the sights and sounds of television are a time of spiritual conflict. A way of seeing reality apart from God is contending with the truth of revelation. The prize is our minds.

The conflict we are caught up in, for the most part unwittingly, is a conflict between the world and the kingdom of God. This is the final, irreducible, and unpleasant reality that analysis of the television worldview leads us to confront. Television viewing, which seems like an ordinary and unimportant activity, has an aspect of supreme importance—the shaping of our minds according to the world or the truth. We have no reason to be surprised by this. The Christian view is that life is shot through with mortal combat between God's kingdom and that of his enemy. The Christian ought to expect that what looks normal and routine is often the very place where the battle rages most fiercely. The soft background music and familiar magazines at the abortion clinic waiting room mask the mortal spiritual battle being waged there. The friendliness of the couple who introduce themselves at the cocktail lounge belies the adulterous nature of their holiday. The Christian knows that life is not as normal and routine as it often seems. As Harry Blamires has put it, "Life is an emergency."[4]

The many hours we spend with television are not simply well-earned relaxation, not even merely a relative waste of time. They are the terrain on which a spiritual struggle is fought out, part of the spiritual crisis of daily life which constantly forces us to choose whom we will serve, which God or god we will love.

Muggeridge's accusation that television offends against the first commandment by making graven images might be restated by saying that the medium frequently offends against the great commandment that we should love God with all our mind, heart, and strength. To love, in this sense, does not primarily mean to feel warm toward. It means to cling to, to give ourselves over to, to submit to, to place above all else. To love God with our minds means to have our minds formed by his word, to have our thinking conformed to his way of seeing things. It is precisely with this that television interferes. To spend many hours with the television is to fail to love God. At some point between our turning on the television for a little entertainment after dinner and our turning it off at the end of the evening, we enter a receptive communion with the images and messages of a culture. We begin with relaxing, and end with loving the world.

Part of the problem is that we have lost a sense of how vulnerable our minds can be to the influences of the world. Many Christians of the past would undoubtedly be amazed at the unworried way we expose our minds to the television world. The early Christians, for example, were sensitive to the imaginative power of pagan poetry, drama, and popular entertainments, and they dealt with them cautiously or not at all. Augustine described his interior life as "a limitless forest, full of unexpected dangers"; he was conscious of the complexities of the mind and the unpredictable ways that images and memories can tempt us and lead us astray.[5] While our embrace of the worldliness of television may not be a deliberate turning away from God, we are certainly responsible for our failure to exercise prudence in our relationship with the medium.

To say that Christians should be more alert to the defense of their minds from the mental influence of television is only half the story. We are not fundamentally on the defensive against the world, although defense is sometimes necessary. As Christians we have been caught up in God's transforming work in the world. We are called to be made new and to carry the message of renewal in Christ into the world. By the Holy Spirit, God is making us like himself. He is enabling us to obey the great commandment, which we could never fulfill by ourselves. He is making our minds and hearts new so that we can love him as he deserves.

What he requires is our cooperation. We must turn our minds and hearts to him. We are to "seek the things that are above, where Christ is." This involves allowing God to make his truth present to our minds in many practical ways through what we read, what we watch, what we listen to. Thus he transforms our minds, and we come to view life from the perspective of being in Christ. We come to know God's will. We come to know the height and breadth of God's love. Because heavy involvement with television jeopardizes this process, we need to limit our time spent with it.

NINE

The Second Age: Cable, Satellites, and Videodiscs

IN ITS FIRST AGE, from the 1940s to the 1980s, television deeply implanted itself in our lives. Almost everyone who could get a set—which was virtually everyone—did so and began spending a lot of time viewing. No one knew much about what that might mean for how we live and how we think. Efforts at understanding came later. We discovered that the medium was a complicated addition to our lives. By the time we began seeing the problems, we had already immersed ourselves. We had dived into the water before finding out how strong the current was.

A second age of television is now beginning. In it, the difficulty of wise use in the home will increase. The current will get stronger, so to speak, as television expands its versatility and usefulness. If we found handling the infant and adolescent medium a challenge, we will not find it easier to deal with the experienced, multitalented, strong-minded adult. If we are ever going to work out a Christian approach to television use in the home, now is the time.

Three major developments are currently expanding the range of material available on the set and are laying the groundwork for greater expansion later on: program distribution by satellites, cable television, and videotape and videodisc systems for home use.

Satellite transmission of television programs from networks

to local broadcasters is a wholesaler-retailer transaction. Until now, most of the 700-odd local television stations in the United States have been affiliated with either the ABC, CBS, or NBC network. The local network affiliates have mostly aired their network's offerings, fed over telephone lines or microwave links. If the local stations wanted, they could broadcast locally produced material or material distributed by various syndicates. But since these options were invariably more expensive, the local broadcasters usually went with the network "feed."

Relatively low-cost transmission to local stations via satellites such as Western Union's Westar and RCA's Satcoms are changing this picture. With satellite transmission, local broadcasters who have the reception equipment can choose from a wide menu of programs sent out by enterprises such as the Public Broadcasting Service, the Christian Broadcasting Network, and others. The local broadcasters find that sometimes they are able to strike a better bargain for a particular time slot with one of these syndicates or part-time networks than with their own parent networks. When they do, they naturally decide to broadcast the alternative material received via satellite. As one writer has put it, the affiliates are severing their umbilicus to the networks. As more and more local stations cut the cord, the possible range of programming increases.

The next step, of course, is for satellite pick-up equipment to become available to individuals. At the moment, technical and legal barriers stand in the way of this happening on a wide scale, but will probably be removed eventually. The Communications Satellite Corporation has already proposed to launch a satellite providing direct transmission to home viewers.

While satellite transmission expands the variety of programs local stations may broadcast, cable increases the number of channels the home set can receive. By the early 1980s, after years of expectation, cable became familiar on the American scene. More than twenty-five percent of American homes had cable, and by the end of the decade, it is expected, forty percent of American homes will be plugged in.[1]

Cable, as most people are by now aware, enables customers to

"Sometimes I wish to God we still had the old 19-inch screen."

receive transmissions which would otherwise be beyond their range, plus other local transmissions sent out by the local cable companies themselves, and subscription offerings from syndicates such as Home Box Office, Showtime, and various informational services. By the 1980s some of these offerings, such as Home Box Office, not only became profitable, but also began eroding the three major networks' share of the total television audience.

Cable has staggering possibilities for channel multiplication. Currently many cables can carry only up to thirty-six channels. But experts foresee the replacement of present copper coaxial cables with cables composed of bundles of hair-thin glass fibers. Using light impulses from lasers, such fiber optical cables have already been designed to carry almost 150 channels. In the future they might be made to bring as many as 1000 channels into the home.

One wonders whether it would ever be commercially feasible to make 1000 programs simultaneously available to anyone and, if it were, what ordinary people sitting down for an evening's entertainment could possibly do with all that material. Glancing at one channel per minute it would take a whole waking day just to look through the entire spectrum once. While it is difficult to conceive of 1000, or even 100, entertainment programs broadcast simultaneously through cable into a single home, it is possible to imagine a wide variety of other kinds of programs being transmitted. Various sorts of specialized information which now come through magazines and books might be channeled into the home by cable. The cable's potential for specialization is, in fact, one of its most important possibilities.

In the first age of television, stations found it unprofitable to devote much air time to particular audiences such as Orthodox Jews, school teachers, or lovers of classical music. Broadcast costs for small-audience programs are as great as costs for large audience ones, but small-audience programs do not attract the advertisers who want to reach the maximum number of viewers. Advertisers who might be interested in reaching the smaller audiences—publishers of books for Jews, teachers, and musicians, for instance, cannot afford to advertise their products to the mass market. They want to advertise just to the people who are likely to want their products. And of course the mass market structure of network television leaves no room for people who are particularly interested in certain kinds of programs to pay for them.

Cable, however, alters both sides of the equation. Individual set owners can contract with the cable company to receive certain channels and programs, much like buying a ticket at a football game. This makes it possible for viewers interested in special kinds of programs, producers of these programs, and advertisers of related products to get together. What has been called narrowcasting begins to replace broadcasting. A similar process has occurred in other media. Many general interest magazines and radio stations have been replaced by ones catering to specialized interests.

Paid offerings over cable have proven profitable. At least some specialized audiences are able and willing to pay for certain programs. So far, advertising to specialized audiences assembled for specialized cable programs has not become widespread; but it would be a logical development.

One further aspect of cable gives it possibilities as endless as the possibilities of human communication itself: cable can be two-way. With the appropriate equipment at the home end, the cable subscriber can send as well as receive. This means the ability to interact with stores, banks, brokers, schools, libraries, hospitals, computers, newspapers, and on and on. The hardware and software, and the distribution systems which would make these possibilities economically feasible, are being developed and tested. An experimental system has been in operation in Columbus, Ohio, for several years.

These potential developments of two-way communication bring television to frontiers where it begins to merge with books, newspapers, magazines, the telephone, and the postal system. It leads into issues that are outside the scope of this book. Here we are concerned with how we deal with what comes *into* our home on the television, not with what goes *out* of the home that way. But the prospect of two-way television suggests the breadth and complexity of television's impact on our lives in its second age.

In addition to greater variety, television's new age will also allow us to see what we want to see (within the limits of what is produced) *when* we want to see it. Videotape recorders and players and videodiscs mean freedom from the scheduling of broadcasters and cable transmitters. Not only will we be able to see programs when we choose, but also as many times as we wish.

In the early eighties, videocassette recorders and players and videodisc players are expensive and not standardized. Several incompatible videodisc technologies are in the field, that is, the discs from one system cannot be played on the others. Nevertheless, more than 40,000 cassette and disc programs are already in circulation. The growth rate is expected to be quite rapid. Estimates are that between 1981 and 1985 the number of households with videocassette equipment will rise from three million to twelve million. By 1985, it was expected, fourteen million videodisc machines will be in use.[2]

As the technology becomes standardized, and technical

progress and economies of large-scale production lower the price, these systems will become cheaper and widely available. The variety of material marketed on tape or disc will enormously increase. We will be able to buy individual tapes or discs like books or record albums. Like cable technology, these tape and disc systems will reduce the size of the audience a program must attract in order to be profitable. A national network program might require fifteen million viewers to clear a profit. A subscription cable program might require 1.5 million. A vieo disc might eventually require 15,000. As the size of the individual subaudiences shrinks, the number of producers and products can be expected to rise.

The combined effects of satellites, cable, and home video systems will make the second age of television quite exciting. The new technologies will give television enormously greater potential for good and ill. The change is as great as the transition from steam engines to internal combustion engines, which made possible the progress from steam locomotives to automobiles, trucks, and airplanes.

Detailed predictions about life in the second age of television are impossible to make accurately, but two forecasts can be made fairly safely.

The first prediction is that there will be the good, the bad, and the pornographic. The first age of television was heralded with high promises. Industry pioneer Thomas Hutchinson forecast sunny skies on the home screen. "To get the most out of television you must give it your undivided attention. This means that television programs must be above the entertainment average that radio has set. And they will be."[3] Let Hutchinson's words stand as a warning to anyone who would make optimistic predictions about television. The first age of television brought some good material and a lot of worthless material into our homes.

In other words, the multiplication of cable channels and other developments are very unlikely to alter the overall quality of the program mix. More specialized tastes will be catered to.

Some kinds of smaller-audience programs which are now unprofitable will become profitable. But much of what is profitable now will continue to be so. Greater variety will probably mean a lot more of the same in many more packages, with some specialty items added. The reasons that the expanded medium will not be flooded with new and better programs are basically twofold—because of (1) the audience, and (2) the industry.

1. Technology will not radically change the main reasons that people watch television now. We will still want to be entertained, to relax, to stay in touch. We will still make our viewing decisions more on the basis of our schedule and habits than on the basis of program content. We will still respond primarily to the medium itself rather than to its contents; thus most viewing will be largely mentally passive. These constants add up to the conclusion that entertainment of a popular sort—comedies, adventures, movies, sports—will continue to attract most of our attention, with a small amount going to news-type programs, and very little going to strictly educational or intellectual programs.

After a study of the relaxed, passive mode in which people generally view television, Mihaly Csikszentmihalyi made this forecast: "If television viewing is at present a passive enterprise, the future promises to allow the viewer greater opportunities to interact with and exert control over the TV set and its content. Nonetheless, the results of [my] study suggest that television, in its present form, may frequently be chosen for the very reason that it *is* unchallenging, relaxing, and relatively uninvolving. To be sure, then, much of television watching in the future will still fulfill these same needs for escape and relaxation. Much of its content will go unchanged because there will be continued demand for such experiences."[4] This means that most of what will be transmitted, taped, and put on disc will not be dramatically different from what we have now.

2. The emergence of a more varied assortment of the same kinds of programs is also foreshadowed by the developing business picture in the video field. More than thirty percent of

all cable systems are already owned by companies which have broadcast interests. This leads one observer, Stuart Brotman, to speculate that "broadcasters may successfully preempt competition by continuing to buy into cable companies and to invest heavily in programming for cable and home video [cassettes and discs], in effect playing both ends against the middle." In other words, the new technologies may come to be dominated by the existing organizations and be made outlets for the existing line of products. Or, Brotman continues, "the new cable networks may become so successful that they begin to attract national advertising—and gradually turn into replicas of the kinds of TV they once sought to replace."[5]

So a few hundred directors and writers who live in the Los Angeles area, men and women who have a particular secular perspective on life, will continue to play a major role in designing the views of reality which most television programs present. Thus the conflict between television content and the Christian mind will continue for the foreseeable future.

However, the new television age also presents expanded opportunities and dangers. While the current mix of programs will probably continue to dominate television in slightly varied forms, it will offer possibilities for some radically different programming. The possibility of producing video material for smaller audiences opens the way for Christians to design entertainment, information, and instruction programming. Alongside the reigning secular television industry there can arise an independent stream of video material shaped by Christian perspectives and values. Such efforts in the second age of television may be more successful than in the first age, when the economic demands of large audiences forced most Christian programming into secular molds.

At the same time, of course, ugly and offensive material will become visible. In fact, it has already appeared. By the early 1980s, for example, between twenty-five and fifty percent of all videocassettes sold feature X-rated entertainment—that is, erotic programs showing sexual intercourse. Tony Schwartz, who writes about television for the *New York Times*, reports that "when a separate network devoted to sexually oriented films has been offered through a cable-television system or as a late-night addition to a subscription television service, the percentage of subscribers willing to pay the extra monthly charge regularly exceeds 50 percent, and has reached as high as 95 percent." The 95 percent figure is from my own town, Ann Arbor, Michigan, where one cable service offers soft-porn—nudity without intercourse.

"There is wide agreement," Schwartz writes, "that cable television will ultimately become the largest and most lucrative outlet for sexual entertainment in the home." Most cable system companies are holding back for now. They do not want to jeopardize their public image while they compete to sign up local franchises. When that restraining motive is gone, some observers believe, cable porn will become so big it will put the art theaters out of business.[6]

So the likeliest forecast for the home screen in television's second age is a great expansion of what came before, with openings for some more explicitly and genuinely Christian programs, other specialty items, and some really bad material. Stuart Brotman concludes: "It is difficult not to invent dispiriting scenarios, given commercial television's own history—and the overall performance to date of the alternatives. The new electronic media will probably make money. They may, in the end, add a bit to the general quality of American TV; they may give us, here and there, a few more real choices than we had before."[7] Surely only the naive would argue that we are at last going to enter the golden age of entertainment and information promised when mass commercial television appeared after World War II.

The second overall projection is that in its second age television will have more rather than less impact on our lives that it has had so far. It is virtually certain that television will not play a decreasing role. We have seen that average daily viewing time reached a plateau in the United States around 1970. Possibly the addition of cable, cassette, and disc inputs will not raise our total time with the medium. Even if not, the technologies are very unlikely to decrease our television involvement.

The greater range of programs and the possibility of controlling scheduling ourselves with cassettes and discs enlarge the possibilities that television will penetrate more of our lives. As a friend remarked to me recently, "All those choices! I doubt it will be good for me when I am able to watch the sixth game of the 1977 World Series whenever I want."

The upshot of these peerings into the future is that greatly expanded television technologies will leave us wrestling with all the basic concerns we now have with television. None of our present problems with television are going to vanish. But in its new period television will be even more potent. Current difficulties will be harder to deal with. The sooner we bring television under control in the Christian home the better.

TEN

Controlling Television in the Christian Home

WE HAVE CONSIDERED problems associated with television viewing and have sketched the outlines of a Christian critique. What conclusions can we draw for how to deal with the medium's disadvantages? Television obviously has many benefits too, a point which it did not seem necessary to explore; our viewing habits show that we do not need to be convinced. What then is a Christian approach to television which takes account of both its strengths and weaknesses? How can we use television to enrich rather than impoverish our homes, and our minds?

The key to formulating a Christian approach is to begin with the commandment that we are to love God with all our heart, mind, and strength. To love God with all our heart and strength involves dedicating our entire lives to him and zealously using all our time in his service. To love him with all our mind means seeking to have our minds formed by the truth which he reveals. Deciding to do this is the place to begin redesigning our viewing habits.

The decision to love God with our mind, heart, and strength has three implications for our use of television. First, it means cutting out the ways that television is siphoning our time away from God's service or is forming our minds contrary to the truth. Second, it means learning to use television to support our loving God. Third, it means reinvesting much of our television

time in activities that will better serve God's purposes for us
and will help us develop a Christian mind. In other words,
loving God totally leads to a threefold television agenda:
eliminate harmful uses, develop helpful uses, and find positive
replacements.

Eliminate harmful uses. Many of television's negative effects
on our homes and our minds can be removed simply by greatly
reducing the amount of time we spend watching it. Here are
some steps toward that goal.

Locate the problems. Before we can eliminate harmful ways of
using television in our home we must find out what they are. In
a general way, this book and others like it can aid in doing that.
But we have to get down to specific problems if we are to work
out specific solutions. Each of us must ask ourselves what
particular problems television is causing in our situation.

We might begin by examining the stress points in our home.
What are the chronic difficulties, the constant points of tension?
Perhaps there are disagreements between husband and wife
about money or work, or struggles with the children about free
time or choice of friends. Perhaps insecurities, resentments, or
anxieties flow beneath the surface.

We might ask ourselves to what extent these problems have
developed because we have not been willing to be generous with
our time, to carry out our responsibilities faithfully, to communicate clearly and fully. How often, when these points of
tension appear, do we say or hear things like, "I didn't have the
time," "I'm too busy," or "We didn't have a chance to talk
about it"? To what extent has television been the cause of this?
How might an investment of time contribute to working
through one of these problems between husband and wife, to
reestablishing communication with a son or daughter, to getting
us out of our isolation and boredom? Asking questions like these
may help us pinpoint the actual opportunity costs *we* have been
paying for our hours spent with the television.

Diagnosing the directly harmful influences television is
having on our minds and behavior may be more difficult

because the influences may be subtle and mingled with many other factors. However, speech indicates what is going on inside our heads, so we might look for clues in the language people are using with one another in the home. Do we make snappy put-downs of each other which echo the lines of situation comedies or quick-talking dramatic characters on television? Is our conversation marked by barbed remarks, jokes at each other's expense, disrespect and insensitivity? If we find that adults and children in the home are speaking in ways that more closely resemble the world of television than the world of scripture, we may conclude that television viewing is one of the reasons. And we may conclude that immersing ourselves in the television world is having a similar effect on our minds and on the rest of our behavior.

Ask why. The second step is to examine the causes of our excessive viewing. Are we trying to escape difficulties in our relationships with the people we live with? Are our children having problems in school or with friends that are causing them to withdraw to the comfort of the screen? Are there frustrations in our jobs which are causing us distress? Do our schedules not allow us time for better kinds of recreation? Are we experiencing the difficulties of living alone and having few friends? We may need to look for solutions to these problems before we are able successfully to adjust our viewing habits.

Accurate measurements. It may be helpful to keep a log of our viewing. Putting a diary on the television set and recording when and what we watch may be quite revealing. We may be watching more than we thought. Also, a log may help us see more clearly the times of the day when we are depending on television. Those are the times when we will have to work particularly hard to find substitutes.

The difficult decision. The big step is to decide to reduce the total amount of time we are spending with television. As we poise the blade, ready to slash our viewing time, the hand trembles. We confront external and internal resistance. One of the external obstacles may be that not everyone in the house or apartment is equally enthusiastic about the move. Another might be our reluctance to face the task of planning what will replace our viewing time.

The internal resistance to watching less television comes from our acceptance of some secular assumptions. The society we live in presumes that leisure is in itself one of the highest goals of life. And it believes that liberal amounts of entertainment through the mass media—television, movies, newspapers, magazines (most of which seek to entertain as well as inform)—are an important component of any normal person's life. The media themselves promote this view. Certainly they rarely suggest the opposite. When was the last time, for example, anyone on television said that Americans are entirely too entertained and media-stimulated and ought to get back to waxing the kitchen floor, insulating the attic, and helping the children with their homework? We have been formed in this cultural pattern. We accept it. We *like* to be in touch with what's happening in the secular culture, trivial as well as important. We feel abnormal if we are not.

Certainly entertainment plays a part in life. Leisure and recreation strengthen the bonds between people and refresh us for exertions ahead. But if we take our call from God seriously, we will ask ourselves *how much* leisure, entertainment, and media stimulation we need. How much prepares us for the work to come; how much distracts us from our duties? "The door turns on its hinge," Proverbs says, "the sluggard turns on his bed." Does the modern sluggard turn on his television? To cut out some of our television viewing goes against an entrenched cultural pattern. However, in light of God's expectation that we diligently use all our talents in his service and make the most of our time, it seems clear that as Christians that is exactly what we are supposed to do.

Turn it off for a couple of weeks. This might come as a shock to the system. The advantage, however, is that everyone gets to see that life without television is possible. Two weeks is long enough for people to begin finding other things they are naturally interested in. Then, when television is reintroduced, plans can be made to continue and enlarge on these natural

interests. Also, it is easier to get to a greatly reduced level of viewing if one approaches it from a temporary experience of no television than if one works one's way to the reduction from the customary high level of viewing.

How much? How much television is enough? Some people I know have adopted an hour a day as a guideline; others, two or three hours a week. These seem like reasonable levels.

Should some people stop watching altogether? At least one group of people should seriously consider doing so—those for whom television is simply out of control. Doing without television entirely is far better than not being able to cross one's living room without feeling an irresistible urge to turn on the television. To give it up completely is preferable to spending large amounts of time—almost against one's will—stupefied before the screen. Better to be thought odd by one's friends than to have one's life at the mercy of an electronic master.

Wilderness preserves. In addition to reducing the total amount of time spent with television, it may be helpful to set aside times when television will almost never be watched—a kind of wilderness preserve in the weekly schedule. One such time might be the dinner hour. A family might decide that dinner is a crucial opportunity for everyone to pause together on their way to other things, keep each other up to date on what is happening at work or school, make plans, pray a little, and enjoy each other's company. Television viewing interferes with this; therefore, no television.

The living room or family room itself might be designated a television-free zone. Most homes have one such room which is dominated by a television set. Some people are trading in their massive stationary set for a portable which can be put away in a closet when it is not in use. This helps to get everyone's mind off television when viewing is not scheduled. Of course, if there are additional sets elsewhere in the house, the opportunities for impulse-viewing are increased and a disciplined approach to viewing is more difficult. It makes sense to dispose of the second and third set.

Planning. Making viewing decisions in advance has three advantages. (1) It is an aid to keeping within whatever guideline we have established for total viewing hours per week. We are likely to watch more than we intended if we do not plan in detail. (2) It helps us be more selective. And (3) it reduces the acrimony of disagreements over what should be watched. Last-minute arguments ("But, Dad, the game's on *now!*") are harder on the nerves than discussions held at the beginning of the week.

Children. Harry Waters noted in *Newsweek* a few years ago that "the question for parents no longer is: 'Do you know where your children are tonight?' The question has become: 'Do you know what they are watching, and with whom?' "[1] These, of course, are not the only questions Christian parents ought to be asking, but parents had certainly better know the answers to these.

Some people say that parents should never use television as a babysitter. Strictly speaking, this is unrealistic. Whenever parents are not actually watching with their children, television is in some sense acting as a babysitter. The children are occupied with the television program, and mom and dad are free to do something else. It does not seem reasonable for parents always to be there when their children are viewing. How much Big Bird and Oscar the Grouch can a mother stand?

What does seem important is that parents know what their children are watching. Parents should determine what is acceptable and unacceptable. Turning a child loose with the television with the mere rule that he average no more than an hour a day would be irresponsible, considering what is available to fill the hour. Parents who are serious about their children growing up as Christians will keep an eye on all the major inputs into their children's lives: friends, school, reading material, television, and so on. Television does not affect everyone the same way. The groupings of people we are part of—family, friends, church, profession, and so on—greatly determine the effects the medium has on us. Television's images come directly to our eyes, but their meaning and impact are filtered through the grid of our own views and the views of the people we are associated with.

A wealth of experimental evidence makes it clear that social relationships greatly affect television's influence on us. The research has concentrated on children, but there is no reason to think that the dynamics of influence discovered in children do not hold true in some fashion for adults. Adults, like children, are deeply affected by the views of the people around them— especially the people they live with and watch television with.

An example comes from studies of the effects of children's programs. Controversy surrounds the question of how much programs such as *Sesame Street* actually teach children (or interfere with learning). It does seem, though, that adult involvement plays an important part. Children who have adults around when they are viewing gain more than those who watch without adults.

A study in Mexico City compared the learning advancement of children who watched the Spanish-language *Plaza Sesamo* in a laboratory setting with those who watched it at home. In the laboratory setting the children who watched *Plaza Sesamo* made greater progress than children who viewed cartoons. But children who watched *Plaza Sesamo* in their own homes did no better than the at-home cartoon watchers. After examining and rejecting every conceivable explanation for this puzzling discrepancy, the researchers concluded that the presence of adults in the laboratory setting may have affected how children received the program. "It is fairly obvious," they wrote, "that in the earlier [laboratory] study, more adults attending to the children were present at more times, creating a subtley different atmosphere. . . . Undoubtedly, *Plaza Sesamo* can be made considerably more effective than it is in its standard broadcast form by incorporating some kind of adult reinforcement or guidance."[2]

Similarly, two researchers at Yale University found that the impact of *Mister Roger's Neighborhood* on children's imaginative play varied according to whether the children viewed the program with an adult. When an adult watched with them and afterwards talked about the material, there was a greater change in the children's play.[3]

Many other studies have uncovered a connection between children's personal relationships and the impact television has on their thinking and behavior. Researchers have found that the way parents approach communication and discipline in the family has a strong influence on children's media usage—what kinds of programs they watch, whether they read newspapers, and so on.[4] Whether children think that their parents and friends regard television material as realistic, it has been shown, is a major factor in whether children think it is realistic.[5] The likelihood that children will be influenced by commercials is related to whether parents are present or absent; the more parents are present during viewing, the weaker the impression made by advertising. Other factors that influence children's susceptibility to commercials are their parents' educational level (the higher the parents' level of education, the lower the children's response to commercials) and the strength of children's friendships (the more integrated children are in a peer group, the less they are affected by the commercials).[6] Some researchers think that television may have little effect on children's values in families where the parents unambiguously make their own values known to counteract what is seen on the screen.[7]

All these studies point to a general conclusion. The more isolated children are from parents and friends, the greater the impact of television on their thinking. The clearer and stronger the influence of parents and peers, the less television influences children.

After referring to a study which showed that children's

political views are molded more by their parents' political views than by the stance of people on television, George Comstock wrote:

> The implication that parents, teachers, and others with some claim to authority can be decisive in a rivalry with television has much that can be said in its behalf. . . . In those surveys in the Surgeon General's inquiry, the positive association between the regular viewing of violent programming and aggressiveness was markedly lower among families where peaceful, nonaggressive means of conflict resolution were emphasized. Adult expressions of opinion, conviction, and judgment, in effect, stand in parallel to firsthand experience—they are a standard in the immediate environment by which a young person can measure the message of a mass medium.
>
> Thus, the question of the influence of television on children and adolescents attracts attention not only to television and what can or should be done about it, but also to the fabric of the society that sits as its audience and to the capability of that society to offer its youth something in addition to and sensitively corrective of television.[8]

Comstock is saying that our personal relationships form the matrix in which we develop our views of the world and our ways of dealing with other people. This is as true in the television age as it has ever been. As Christians we should not be surprised to hear a social scientist saying so. Scripture plainly teaches that the place where God reshapes our lives is the body of believers. It is as members of the church that we come to know the height and length and breadth of God's love and come to human maturity in Christ. It is within the body of Christ that we find the instruction, discipline, example, and support that enable us to grow to be the men and women God intends us to become.

Comstock underlines an important point. If we are to control television and use it wisely, we must do more than twist the on-off knob and the channel selector. We need to *be* the kinds of families and local church bodies which influence each other toward God's ways and strengthen each other to resist those aspects of the television worldview which are "the world" in the sense of human society apart from God.

Practically, this means being families where God's word is spoken and discussed, where un-Christian ideas are actively identified and countered with the truth. St. Paul, who gave an example of this active confrontation with falsehood in his life and writings, epitomized the approach we need to take when he said, "We destroy arguments and every proud obstacle to the knowledge of God, and take every thought captive to obey Christ."

But we need to do much more than cultivate Christian thinking and conversation and actively teach our children. The studies cited show that *the ways we relate* as family members have an important effect on television's impact on us. The scriptural teaching is not that we should merely be sharp in recognizing and countering falsehood. It is that we should set a priority on our *relationships as Christians*—husbands and wives, parents and children, brothers and sisters in Christ. Strengthening our relationships as Christians—building strong families and local church communities—even in ways that have no connection to television, in the long run is crucial to our being able to deal with television in a positive way. Christians in strong homes and churches have a base from which to use television. They are in a position to use television moderately without anxiety. The more isolated, estranged, separated, and at odds with one another we are and the less cohesive our family and church life is, the more vulnerable we will be to the shaping influences of television.

From this principle we may draw two conclusions. The first, clearly, is that we must begin not with television but, to use George Comstock's words, with "the fabric of society," with our personal relationships with one another as Christians. Without strength here, television and other secular influences will ultimately be the major influences on our lives.

Second, we ought to work at learning how to actively confront the secular messages and models that television and the other media present to us. We ought to have it as a goal to develop our thinking and patterns of conversation to explicitly counterbalance secular influences such as television's.

We will be best able to make television viewing a positive and useful experience if we view it with other people. Solitary viewing leaves us alone with television's influences. These influences are magnified for us when we view alone because the isolated viewer tends to become passive. By contrast, if we work to make it so, watching with other people can be a more active experience. We can develop habits of discussing what we are seeing, good and bad, in ways that heighten our understanding of the moral and other issues involved.

Parents can use television, to some extent, for teaching. Some programs can be used as a springboard for discussion. One goal is to help children gain a better perspective on programs they are attracted to but which have serious problems. Another goal is to use good programs as an opportunity for teaching, capitalizing on the fact that children would rather watch television than listen to a lecture.

While it is possible to make positive use of television, it is not easy. Among the pitfalls are these five:

1. Television is fascinating. The screen itself, regardless of what in particular is on it, is very attractive to the eye, for reasons that are not well understood. Video displays affect the eye's focusing mechanisms in ways that make the screen particularly interesting and, at the same time, slightly visually disorienting.[9] We are dealing with a medium which, for physiological reasons, has some hidden resistances to any rational plan to control it.

2. Watching television is easier to do than almost anything else. It is even easier than daydreaming, because it produces our fantasies for us. Given the path-of-least-resistance tendency which we all seem to have in some measure, television's easiness makes it an adversary of our will. Give television an inch, and it tries to take a yard. Many are the men and women who sat down to watch a half-hour program and stayed the evening.

3. Television viewing tends strongly toward mental passivity.

Despite our best intentions, the dynamics of viewing seem to normally flow downhill to the level of least mental alertness, no matter whether we are watching cops and robbers or a presidential resignation speech. The viewer who comes determined not to be lulled should realize he has a struggle on his hands.

4. We can easily overestimate our ability to confront television's non-Christian viewpoints. "Oh, it won't affect *me*," is a widespread and presumptuous attitude. A more realistic attitude is to see ourselves, as members of the human race, as susceptible to certain kinds of influence. A corollary is not to overestimate our ability to counteract the influence of television's non-Christian influences on our children. Let each of us soberly assess our teaching abilities—and our children's impressionability.

5. Finally, the possibilities of television-plus-discussion as a teaching tool are limited. There *are* some people who think the possibilities are limitless. Simply sit down next to the children, turn on the set, and parents and children are off on a roller-coaster ride through current events and value clarification. Barbara Harrison writes: "Even the worst television programs— sometimes, oddly enough, *especially* the worst television programs—create the opportunity for children to develop moral and aesthetic judgments and choices. I'd just as soon they explored and defined and articulated their feelings in our living room before they test them out—or are themselves tested—in the world. And I want to be there with them while they're doing it."[10] There is some point to what Harrison says, but plainly this kind of thing can be overdone. Not only is television fascinating and so on, but also as a teaching tool it is not in the parents' control. It is an unpredictable and volatile curriculum.

Frank Mankiewicz and Joel Swerdlow offer this example:

Consider the routine programming decision made in 1975 by the producers of *All in the Family*. It was decided that on a given Monday night . . . Archie Bunker's daughter would announce her pregnancy to her husband. It would appear that conception had occurred during the weekend when the daughter had left her "pills" at home—perhaps, her husband thought, deliberately. Her husband, at first pleased, then accused his wife of deliberately leaving the pills at home and of "seducing" him by wearing a bikini. The daughter charged, "You could have taken a cold shower," to which her husband replied, "I did take a cold shower." The topper for this sequence was then the daughter's line, "Yes, but you took it with me." In the next scene the daughter and her mother discuss the pregnancy and the possibility of an abortion. . . .

As soon as the program entered millions of living rooms, millions of American parents had to face children's questions about abortion, conception, and, perhaps, the role of cold showers in this process. It is quite likely that many parents handled this well, and it is also quite likely that many did not. But the producers of *All in the Family* decided for both sets of parents when they would discuss these problems with their children.[11]

The unpredictability of television material can be somewhat controlled by planning with *TV Guide* or a similar listing that offers program descriptions. But even then, one is often surprised. (Cassettes and discs will make it possible for parents to view programs before their children do—if they will actually take the time to do it.)

The upshot of all these cautions is to say that while television can be used well, it is not an easy creature to tame. It is not, for the most part, designed to provide entertaining and informative social occasions, to be a foil for Christian commentary, or to be an instructional tool for Christian parents. It is designed to fascinate, to keep our heads turned to the screen, to sell products. It does what it sets out to do very well. Anyone who would use secular television programming for constructive purposes has a considerable challenge on their hands.

The situation is similar to that of the man who took a liking to a stray dog. The dog had its lovable points, but it had never been trained and now was old and set in its ways. The man established some rules that made it possible to have the dog in the house for periods of time without anything getting damaged. But the animal was not well-mannered enough to become a house pet. The best arrangement, the man found, was to keep it outside most of the time. The relationship worked well because the man appreciated the dog's good points but was also a shrewd judge of canine nature and knew how to take a strong hand when necessary.

Finding positive replacements. Giving something up is always easier if we have something good to put in its place. That is a practical reason for giving thought to what activities we will replace some of our television time with. But why do we want to watch less television in the first place if not to have more time to do more of the things we should be doing. In a sense, then, we are not looking for television substitutes. We are clearing away some of our viewing so we can get on with the activities that we have responsibility for—caring for our spouse, children, relatives, friends, fellow church members, neighbors, people in need, and so on.

One particular kind of activity can be recommended—an effort to grow in developing a Christian mind. For example, if a person does not read scripture at least a few times during the week, establishing such a pattern is a good place to start. A person might make at least one clear decision to do something additional to cooperate with the Holy Spirit in developing a greater daily awareness of Christian truth—a regular effort to be reading Christian books and magazines, listening to tapes of Christian teaching or preaching, or listening to a religious radio program. Parents might also decide to begin some religious instruction with their children, perhaps by setting aside an evening a week for teaching and reading aloud.

Television will only have a useful, balanced role in our lives if we are doing the other things we need to in order to carry out our responsibilities and have our minds shaped according to God's word. Reducing our viewing time and changing some of our viewing habits are part of the movement toward balance. The other part consists of the positive changes we make to dedicate our time to fulfilling God's purposes and understanding his ways.

Making changes in our television viewing may seem reasonable but difficult. Here are three suggestions for how to go about it successfully.

1. Repent. For many of us, getting control of television must begin with our recognizing that our viewing habits are as dissatisfying to God as they are to us. Letting our time get away from us, failing to carry out our responsibilities diligently, allowing our minds to be formed by the secular culture—none of this pleases him. Whatever is displeasing to God in our lives is matter for repentance. That means seeing clearly what we are doing wrong, acknowledging it to God and asking his forgiveness, and determining with his help to do differently.

More than 6,000 books have been written about television, many of them critical. Almost every other issue of the daily newspaper, it seems, carries an article about the problems of television. Comic strips are full of jibes at what's on and how passively we watch it. We have become familiar with the problems of television viewing. Each of us develops our personal collection of complaints about the medium. We each know what we think is wrong with television and our viewing habits, and we readily share our observations with one another. Dissatisfaction with television and uneasiness about our relationship with it are national cultural traits.

Yet there has been no discernible popular movement away from heavy involvement with television. We criticize the medium, and ourselves for spending so many hours with it, but we have not taken the matter seriously enough to make a decisive change. We have not yet repented.

2. Ask God's help. If we are making a change in response to what we believe God wants of us, we can rely on him to give us the power to do it.

It would be a mistake to adopt a mainly defensive attitude

regarding television. We do need to defend ourselves against many of its influences. We do need to free a good deal of the time which we regularly invest in television. The right perspective, however, is not that we are on the defensive. Rather we should see that there is a spiritual struggle going on between men and women who have committed their minds, hearts, and strength to the Lord, and the world which seeks to pry us loose from that commitment. Our mundane little difficulties with altering our viewing habits are part of a much larger struggle going on between the kingdom of God and the kingdom of his enemy. But the one with whom we are aligned, the Lord himself, has overcome the world. In union with him, we can overcome it too. In him, we have the power and freedom we need to make the changes we ought to make.

3. Find other Christians who are moving in the same direction, and support one another. Because changing television habits runs in the face of cultural trends, it helps to do it with at least a few other people. Controlling television is only one of the many reasons why Christian families and single people should find ways of sharing their lives more and supporting each other in the difficult areas of daily life. But certainly the challenge of television is one reason to do this.

A group of Christians might decide to get together once a week for a few months to discuss their thoughts about television and what they each feel called to do. They could hold themselves accountable to the group for keeping decisions each has made regarding a change in viewing habits. Beyond this, there is the possibility that a group of Christians would decide to do some things together in replacement of some of their television viewing. For example, some Christian families spend Saturday evenings together regularly, taking a little time for prayer, having a meal, playing games, reading aloud to one another, and so on.

Christians can take three routes to the control of television. All are important; all should be taken.

The first route is to bring pressure to bear on those who

produce, transmit, and pay for the programs, demanding that they eliminate objectionable material. This can be done by legislation and ordinances which, for instance, prevent hard or soft pornography from being delivered over cable systems franchised by the local government. It can be done by expressions of widespread displeasure brought to the attention of the networks and local broadcasters. It can be done by boycotting advertisers who pay for objectionable programs.

All of these are perfectly legitimate. Local communities have the right to determine what kinds of material do not meet community standards. Whether material violates community standards is, in fact, the question the Supreme Court asks when determining if material is pornographic. Similarly, expressions of protest to networks, broadcasters, and advertisers alert them to the views of the people they claim to be serving. Nothing could be more appropriate than those being served making their views known clearly.

Some people object that boycotting of advertisers is censorship. Censorship is government control of what is published or broadcast. Boycotting is simply people voting with their wallets. The message to the advertiser is, "I object to the material you are paying to have aired. I, for one, won't give you my business if you continue to offend me this way." Donald Wildmon, leader of one movement which has organized advertiser boycotts, has commented that when people are not free to spend their money where they want, then we will no longer have any real freedom.

Boycotts are a more popular expression of views about television content than the system of selection which now prevails. The few hundred people who write, produce, and schedule network programming are a handful compared to the thousands of people who have organized in recent years to fight for the removal of offensive material.

It is reasonable for Christians to take a concern for the civil society of which they are part. Television and the images it distributes to the entire nation is our most public institution. It is, as we have seen, the popular mediator of the perspectives and values of contemporary society. There is a clear responsibility for Christians to be involved in setting limits beyond which the industry may not go—limits regarding such things as blasphemy, sexual indecency, and extreme forms of violence and cruelty.

The second route to the proper control of television is more positive. It involves not what should be removed but what should be put in view. Christians should be concerned that television is used to transmit views of reality and models of behavior which are consonant with reality as God has revealed it to be and with the life he calls men and women to live. This means that there is a need for both explicitly Christian programs and also a Christian influence in the entire industry which produces secular news and entertainment. How Christians might effectively penetrate and work within the social environments where the television world is created is a very difficult problem. In many ways these environments are among the most resistant in our society to the message and outlook of the gospel. The technological changes that are underway do, however, hold out the opportunity for a greater variety of genuinely Christian programs being produced.

The third route is that explored in this book—control at the home end. Even if all the objectionable material were taken off the air and out of the cables, and more genuinely good material were available, control in the home would still be necessary.

People tend to treat television as a utility. With utilities we generally concern ourselves with steady availability, quality, and cost. For instance, we want to know that whenever we turn on the faucet water—clean water—will come out. After all, we use water all the time. This, unfortunately, is how many people think of television. They use it all the time; they have no intention of using less. They simply want to know that what they are getting is not dangerous. But we ought to treat television not as a utility but as a product or service. Products and services must be chosen. Even if all the programming were fair to good, the need to select would remain, as would the need to be active and critical in our use of it.

Television is similar to many other innovations of the modern age. It appeared suddenly and quickly established itself everywhere. Life without it became unthinkable. The same had happened with the locomotive, the automobile, and so on. The pattern is that *after* the innovation becomes universal and indispensable, the disadvantages and problems begin to appear.

Sometimes the problems are enormous. The automobile, for example, has dealt what may be a fatal blow to the large old cities of the northeast United States. The entire industrial system, it has become clear, is taxing the natural environment beyond its capacity to sustain indefinitely. Television, it turns out, has its drawbacks too. They tend to be more subtle, and they come more pleasantly wrapped, but they are real problems nonetheless. Now, with these problems still unresolved, the technology is rocketing everyone into a second television revolution.

With all the modern innovations, eventually the troublesome byproducts and side effects must be faced. In the case of television, the time has long since come. For half a generation Christians have urgently needed to take control of television in their own homes.

While readjusting our television habits may be difficult, it is not actually impossible. It may be impossible to restore the huge old industrial cities to health; it may be impossible to reverse the chronic strains of industrial society on the environment. It is not, however, impossible to control television in the Christian home.

Very well, let us do it.

Notes

Introduction
Time To Take Stock

1. Virginia Stem Owens, *The Total Image, Or Selling Jesus in the Modern Age* (Grand Rapids, Mich.: Eerdmans, 1980).

Chapter One
Paying with Our Time

1. Eli A. Rubenstein, George A. Comstock, and John P. Murray, eds., *Television and Social Behavior* (Washington, D.C.: U.S. Government Printing Office, 1972), five volumes.

2. Cited by Neil P. Hurley, "The 'Drop-Ins': Mass Media and the Poor," *America,* Nov. 26, 1977, p. 377.

3. John P. Robinson, "Television and Leisure Time: Yesterday, Today, and (Maybe) Tomorrow," *Public Opinion Quarterly* 33 (1969), pp. 210-222.

4. Polls by Peter D. Hart Associates, cited by Dennis Meredith, "Future World of Television—Another 'Revolution' Coming," *Science Digest,* Sept. 1980, p. 21.

5. R.T. Bower, *Television and the Public* (New York: Holt, Rinehart, and Winston, 1973), summarized in George A. Comstock, ed., *Television and Human Behavior: The Key Studies* (Santa Monica, Calif.: The Rand Corporation, 1975), p. 125.

6. Judith K. Walters and Vernon A. Stone, "Television and Family Communication," *Journal of Broadcasting* 15 (1971), pp. 409-414.

7. John P. Robinson, "Toward Defining the Functions of Television," in Rubenstein, *et al.,* eds., *op. cit.,* Volume 4, pp. 577-578.

8. Mihaly Csikszentmihalyi and Robert Kubey, "Television and the Rest of Life: A Systematic Comparison of Subjective Experience," *Public Opinion Quarterly* 45 (1981), pp. 317-338.

Chapter Two
Displacement Effects

1. P. Wilson, "In Praise of the Television Addicts," *The Boston Globe,* July 14, 1974, p. 6a.

2. John P. Robinson, "Television's Impact on Everyday Life: Some Crossnational Evidence," in Rubenstein, *et al.,* eds., *op. cit.,* Volume 4, p. 411.

3. W.A. Belson, "Effects of Television on the Interests and Initiative of Adult Viewers in Greater London," *British Journal of Psychology* 50 (1959), pp. 145-158; Cunningham and Walsh, *Videotown: 1948-1958* (New York: Cunningham and Walsh, 1959).

4. John P. Robinson, "Toward Defining the Functions of Television," in Rubenstein, *et al.*, eds., *op cit.*, Volume 4, p. 579.

5. Alexis S. Tan, "Why TV Is Missed: A Functional Analysis," *Journal of Broadcasting* 21 (1977), p. 376.

6. Leo B. Hendry and Helen Patrick, "Adolescents and Television," *Journal of Youth and Adolescence* 6 (1977), pp. 325-336.

7. Kas Kalba, "The Electronic Community," in Douglass Cater and Richard Adler, eds., *Television As a Social Force*, (New York: Praeger, 1975), p. 145.

8. Marie Winn, *The Plug-In Drug* (New York: Viking, 1977), pp. 114-115.

9. *Ibid.*, pp. 161-162.

10. "Learning Less," *Time*, March 31, 1975, p. 67.

11. "Academic Slump Hits Whiz Kids, Too," *U.S. News and World Report*, March 16, 1981, p. 12.

12. "Learning Less," *Time*, March 31, 1975, p. 67.

13. Robert C. Hornik, "Television Access and the Slowing of Cognitive Growth," *American Educational Research Journal* 15 (1978), pp. 1-15.

14. For a summary see George Comstock, Steven Chaffee, Natan Katzman, Maxwell McCombs, and Donald Roberts, *Television and Human Behavior* (New York: Columbia University Press, 1978), pp. 179-180.

15. Leo B. Hendry and Helen Patrick, *op. cit.*

16. Takeo Furu, *et al.*, *The Function of Television for Children and Adolescents* (Tokyo: Monumenta Nipponica, 1971).

17. Robert C. Hornik, *op. cit.*

18. George Comstock, *et al.*, *op, cit.*, pp. 179-180.

19. Robert C. Hornik, *op. cit.*

Chapter Three
The Empty Experience

1. Thomas H. Hutchinson, *Here Is Television* (New York: Hastings House, 1946), pp. ix-xi.

2. The quotations are from Marilyn Preston, "How I Love—Chomp, Chomp—to Watch TV," *The Detroit Free Press*, Aug. 3, 1980; some of the findings are reported by Mihaly Csikszentmihalyi and Robert Kubey, *op. cit.*

3. John P. Robinson, "Toward Defining the Functions of Television," in Rubenstein, *et al.*, eds., *op. cit.*, Volume 4, pp. 576-577.

4. Quoted in Jerry Mander, *Four Arguments for the Elimination of Television* (New York: Morrow Quill, 1978), p. 209; see also Thomas B. Mulholland and Erik Peper, "Occipital Alpha and Accomodative Vergence, Pursuit Tracking, and Fast Eye Movements," *Psychophysiology* 8 (1971), pp. 556-575.

5. Herbert E. Krugman, "Brain Wave Measures of Media Involvement,"

Journal of Advertising Research, Feb. 1971, pp. 3-9.

6. Herbert E. Krugman and E.L. Hartley, "Passive Learning from Television," *Public Opinion Quarterly* 34 (1970), pp. 184-190.

Chapter Four
Television and Our Thinking

1. George Comstock, *et al., op. cit.,* p. xiii.

2. Howard Gardner, "Reprogramming the Media Researchers," *Psychology Today,* Jan. 1980, p. 6.

3. Neil Postman, "TV's 'Disastrous' Impact on Children," *U.S. News and World Report,* Jan. 19, 1981.

4. Christine L. Nystrom, "Immediate Man," *Et cetera,* March 1977; the quotations which follow are from pp. 25-28.

5. George Will, "Responsibility in Journalism," *New Wine,* July-August 1981, p. 28.

6. Neil Postman, *op. cit.,* pp. 43-44.

7. Michael Novak, "Television Shapes the Soul," in Douglass Cater and Richard Allen, eds., *op. cit.,* p. 12.

8. Described by Howard Gardner, *op. cit.,* pp. 12-13.

9. *Ibid.*

Chapter Five
A Curious Access to Our Minds

1. George Gerbner and Larry Gross, "Living with Television: The Violence Profile," *Journal of Communication* 26 (1976), pp. 178-179.

2. Russell Baker, "As the World Turns," *The (Compact) New York Times,* Oct. 30, 1977, p. 136.

3. George Will, "The Not-So-Mighty Tube," *Newsweek,* Aug. 8, 1977, p. 34.

4. Dennis Meredith, *op. cit.,* p. 21.

5. Alberta E. Siegel, "Communicating with the Next Generation," *Journal of Communication* 25 (1975), p. 19.

Chapter Six
Arousal, Role Models, and Behavior Modification

1. F. Scott Andison, "TV Violence and Viewer Aggression: A Cumulation of Study Results, 1956-1976," *Public Opinion Quarterly,* 41 (1977), p. 323.

2. David Loye, "TV's Impact on Adults: It's Not All Bad News," *Psychology Today,* May 1978, pp. 87-94.

3. Richard A. Dienstbier, "Sex and Violence: Can Research Have It Both Ways?" *Journal of Communication* 27 (1977), p. 179.

4. *Ibid.,* p. 182.

5. Gaye Tuchman, "Mass Media Values," *Society,* Nov.-Dec. 1976, p. 54. For an informative analysis of how television's economic structures determine

programming content, see Rose K. Goldsen, *The Show and Tell Machine: How Television Works and Works You Over* (New York: Dell, 1977).

6. J.A Flanders, "A Review of Research on Imitative Behavior," *Psychological Bulletin* 69 (1968), pp. 316-337; summarized in George A. Comstock, ed., *Television and Human Behavior: The Key Studies,* (Santa Monica, Calif.: The Rand Corporation, 1975), p. 150.

7. S. Feshbach, "Reality and Fantasy in Filmed Violence," in Rubenstein, *et al.,* eds., *op. cit.,* Volume 2, pp. 318-345.

8. Fern L. Johnson and Leslie K. Davis, "Hesitation Phenomena in the Language of Family Conversational Styles in Three Formats of Television Programming in the U.S.A.," paper presented at the Ninth World Congress of the International Sociological Association, 1978.

9. R.E.A. Goranson, "A Review of Recent Literature on Psychological Effects of Media Portrayals of Violence," in R.K. Baker and S.J. Ball, eds., *Violence and the Media: A Staff Report to the National Commission on the Causes and Prevention of Violence* (Washington, D.C.: U.S. Government Printing Office, 1969), pp. 395-413.

10. Albert Bandura, "Influence of Models' Reinforcement Contingencies on the Acquisition of Imitative Responses," *Journal of Personality and Social Psychology* 1 (1965), pp. 589-595.

11. M. Mark Miller and Byron Reeves, "Dramatic TV Content and Children's Sex-Role Stereotypes," *Journal of Broadcasting* 20 (1976), pp. 47, 49.

12. Michael J. Robinson, "Prime Time Chic: Between Newsbreaks and Commercials, the Values Are L.A. Liberal," *Public Opinion,* March-May 1979, pp. 42-48.

13. *Ibid.*

14. *Ibid.*

15. Rose K. Goldsen, *op. cit.,* pp. 16-27.

16. *Ibid.*

Chapter Seven
The Video View of Life

1. George Gerbner and Larry Gross, *op. cit.,* p. 180.

2. George Gerbner and his colleagues have created a considerable literature on the shape of the television world and its impact on viewers' perspectives on reality. A popular explanation of their research appeared in George Gerbner and Larry Gross, "The Scary World of TV's Heavy Viewer," *Psychology Today,* April 1976, pp. 41ff. The team has published annual reports for more than a decade in the *Journal of Communication.* The references concerning their theories of mainstreaming and resonance are to George Gerbner, Larry Gross, Michael Morgan, and Nancy Signorelli, "The 'Mainstreaming' of America: Violence Profile No. 11," *Journal of Communication* 30 (1980), pp. 10-29.

3. Melvin L. DeFleur and L.B. DeFleur, "The Relative Contribution of

Television As a Learning Source for Children's Occupational Knowledge," *American Sociological Review* 32 (1967), pp. 777-789.

4. George Comstock, *et al., op. cit.,* p. 15.

5. Frank Mankiewicz and Joel Swerdlow, *Remote Control: Television and the Manipulation of American Life* (New York: Times Books, 1978), p. 53.

6. Stanley J. Brown, "How TV and Film Portrayals Affect Sexual Satisfaction in College Students," *Journalism Quarterly* 53 (1976), pp. 468-473.

7. George Gerbner, *et al.,* "The 'Mainstreaming' of America: Violence Profile No. 11," *Journal of Communication* 30 (1980), p. 14.

8. George Gerbner, "Cultural Indicators: The Case of Violence in Television Drama," *Annals of the American Academy of Political and Social Science* 338 (1970), pp. 69-81.

9. An introduction to the various levels of meaning in television's programming is John Fiske and John Hartley, *Reading Television* (London: Methuen, 1978).

10. Ben Stein, *The View from Sunset Boulevard: America As Brought to You by the People Who Make Television* (New York: Basic Books, 1979).

Chapter Eight
Television and the Christian Mind

1. Peggy J. West, *Growing with Television; Adult Learner's Guide and Resources for Participants* (New York: Seabury, 1980).

2. Malcolm Muggeridge, "Will Faith Spoil Malcolm Muggeridge?" interview, *U.S. Catholic,* Nov. 1979, p. 28.

3. Malcolm Muggeridge, *Christ and the Media* (Grand Rapids, Mich.: Eerdmans, 1977).

4. Harry Blamires presents a penetrating analysis of the clash of secularist and Christian thinking in *The Secularist Heresy* [originally *The Faith and Modern Error*] (Ann Arbor, Mich.: Servant, 1981). He calls for the restoration of a genuinely Christian mentality in *The Christian Mind* (Ann Arbor, Mich.: Servant, 1978).

5. Augustine, *The Confessions,* X, xxxv.

Chapter Nine
The Second Age: Cable, Satellites, and Videodiscs

1. Harry F. Waters, *et al.,* "Cable TV: Coming of Age," *Newsweek,* Aug. 24, 1981, pp. 45, 47.

2. James L. Hodge, "Mass Media: Ramifications of the Coming Revolution," *Christianity Today,* June 26, 1981, p. 21.

3. Thomas Hutchinson, *op. cit.*

4. Mihaly Csikszentmihalyi and Robert Kubey, *op. cit.,* p. 326.

5. Stuart N. Brotman, "The New Era," *The Wilson Quarterly* 5 (1981), p. 85.

6. Tony Schwartz, "The TV Pornography Boom," *The New York Times Magazine*, Sept. 13, 1981, pp. 44ff.

7. Stuart N. Brotman, *op. cit.*, p. 85.

Chapter Ten
Controlling Television in the Christian Home

1. Harry F. Waters, "What TV Does to Kids," *Newsweek*, Feb. 21, 1977, p. 70.

2. Rogelio Diaz-Guerrero, Isabel Reyes-Lagunes, Donald B. Witzke, and Wayne H. Holtzman, "*Plaza Sesamo* in Mexico: An Evaluation," *Journal of Communication* 26 (1976), pp. 145-154.

3. Jerome L. Singer and Dorothy G. Singer, "Can TV Stimulate Imaginative Play?" *Journal of Communication* 26 (1976), pp. 74-80.

4. Jack McLeod and Garrett J. O'Keefe, Jr., "The Socialization Perspective and Communications Behavior," in F. Gerald Kline and Phillip J. Tichenor, eds., *Current Perspectives in Mass Communications Research* (Beverly Hills, Calif.: Sage, 1972).

5. B.S. Greenberg and B. Reeves, "Children and the Perceived Reality of Television," summarized in George Comstock, ed., *Television and Human Behavior: The Key Studies*, (Santa Monica, Calif.: The Rand Corporation, 1975), p. 161.

6. Thomas S. Robertson and John R. Rossiter, "Children's Responsiveness to Commercials," *Journal of Communication* 27 (1977), pp. 101-106.

7. Ellen E. Maccoby, "Effects of the Mass Media," in M. Hoffman and L.W. Hoffman, eds., *Review of Child Development Research*, Volume 1 (New York: Russell Sage Foundation, 1964), pp. 323-348.

8. George Comstock, "Television Entertainment: Taking It Seriously," *Character*, Oct. 1980, pp. 7-8.

9. See Marie Winn, *op. cit.*

10. Barbara G. Harrison, "How TV Can Be Good for Children," *McCall's*, Oct. 1977, p. 165.

11. Frank Mankiewicz and Joel Swerdlow, *op. cit.*, p. 202.